The BERA Guide to Outdoor Learning

'The *BERA Guide to Outdoor Learning: Place-responsive Pedagogy in Educational Research and Practice* offers an inspiring exploration of outdoor education through the lens of place-responsiveness. It is a timely and welcome contribution to the growing literature on outdoor learning that underscores the importance of taking education outdoors to provide children and young people with opportunities to directly engage and interact with the world around them. Organised in two parts, the book first blends theoretical insights with practical advice for place-pedagogy before moving on to provide examples of place-based pedagogy in action. With a commitment to experiential learning, this book challenges practitioners to slow down and thoughtfully engage students with their locality thus embracing outdoor learning as a transformative approach to embrace the transformative power of outdoor learning to cultivate deeper connections with place, community and self through place-responsive pedagogy. It is both a call to action and a reflective guide for those seeking to create meaningful, holistic educational experiences beyond the classroom.'

– Dr Emma Rawlings Smith, Lecturer in Sustainability and Geography Education, University of Southampton, UK

'We cannot underestimate the importance of Outdoor Learning in our primary schools. From Early Years mud kitchens to Upper Key Stage Two outdoor and adventurous residentials, the aims remain the same: to be active in the fresh air and feel good; to embrace new experiences and surprise ourselves; to exist in the moment and feel connected to our surroundings; to take notice and remember the simple things that give us joy. This book is essential reading for all educators who want to spread the word, reshape the curriculum and in doing so change young lives for the better.'

– Mrs Jo Colledge, Headteacher, Ingleton Primary School, UK

The BERA Guides

Critical Insights into Educational Research and Practice

About the series

Published in partnership between the British Educational Research Association and Emerald Publishing, *The BERA Guides* are short, research-informed yet accessible introductions to key, interdisciplinary topics impacting education research and practice.

Books in the series present a summary of the research on the topic, charting how scholarly thought and practice have evolved over time, and offering critical takeaways and suggestions for future work within and beyond academia. With the guides viewed as 'primers' on each topic, the series is for use by a broad academic audience, including early career and established researchers, postgraduate students and practitioners.

Previously published in the series

The BERA Guide to Mental Health and Wellbeing in Schools: Exploring Frontline Support in Educational Research and Practice; *Edited by Michelle Jayman, Jonathan Glazzard, Anthea Rose and Aimee Quickfall*

The BERA Guide to Decolonising the Curriculum: Equity and Inclusion in Educational Research and Practice; *Edited by Marlon Lee Moncrieffe, Omolabake Fakunle, Marlies Kustatscher and Anna Olsson Rost*

Forthcoming in the series

The BERA Guide to Practitioner Research: Developing Professional Knowledge in Educational Research and Practice; *Edited by Kate Mawson, Claire Tyson, Tom Perry and Joyce I-Hui Chen*

The BERA Guide to Climate Change Education: Systemic Approaches in Educational Research and Practice; *Authored by Dima Khazem*

The BERA Guide to Implementing Inclusive Education: Understanding SEND in UK Educational Research and Practice; *Edited by Rhiannon Packer*

The BERA Guide to Environmental and Sustainability Education: Creating just futures in Educational Research and Practice; *Edited by Elizabeth Rushton and Lynda Dunlop*

The BERA Guide to Social Justice-Oriented Leadership: Connections and Implications in Educational Research and Practice; *Authored by Liliana Belkin and Deborah A. Sabric*

The BERA Guide to Outdoor Learning

Place-responsive Pedagogy in Educational Research and Practice

Edited by

Lucy Sors
York St John University, UK

and

Ruth Unsworth
University of Glasgow, UK

United Kingdom – North America – Japan – India
Malaysia – China

Emerald Publishing Limited
Emerald Publishing, Floor 5, Northspring, 21-23 Wellington Street, Leeds LS1 4DL.

First edition 2025

Editorial matter and selection © 2025 Lucy Sors and Ruth Unsworth.
Individual chapters © 2025 The authors.
Published under exclusive licence by Emerald Publishing Limited.

Reprints and permissions service
Contact: www.copyright.com

No part of this book may be reproduced, stored in a retrieval system, transmitted in any form or by any means electronic, mechanical, photocopying, recording or otherwise without either the prior written permission of the publisher or a licence permitting restricted copying issued in the UK by The Copyright Licensing Agency and in the USA by The Copyright Clearance Center. Any opinions expressed in the chapters are those of the authors. Whilst Emerald makes every effort to ensure the quality and accuracy of its content, Emerald makes no representation implied or otherwise, as to the chapters' suitability and application and disclaims any warranties, express or implied, to their use.

British Library Cataloguing in Publication Data
A catalogue record for this book is available from the British Library

ISBN: 978-1-83608-193-7 (Print)
ISBN: 978-1-83608-190-6 (Online)
ISBN: 978-1-83608-192-0 (Epub)

INVESTOR IN PEOPLE

To our daughters

Contents

List of Figures and Table	xi
About the Editors	xiii
About the Contributors	xv
Foreword	xix
Acknowledgements	xxi

Introduction: Encountering Ideas of Place in Outdoor Learning   1
Lucy Sors and Ruth Unsworth

A Pause for Connection   13
Lucy Sors

PART 1: THEORISING PLACE-RESPONSIVE PEDAGOGY IN OUTDOOR LEARNING

Chapter 1 – Place-responsive Pedagogy in Outdoor Learning   17
Lucy Sors

Chapter 2 – Decolonising Outdoor Learning: Developing Connectedness Through Place-responsive Pedagogy Beyond the Early Years in England   33
Lucy Sors and Louise Whitfield

Chapter 3 – Inclusive and Holistic Practice in Place-responsive Outdoor Learning   53
Lucy Sors

PART 2: PLACE-RESPONSIVE PEDAGOGY IN ACTION

Chapter 4 – Building Connection to Place: Time and Space in Place-responsive Pedagogy   85
Ruth Unsworth

Chapter 5 – Mudfulness? Nurturing a Relationship with Nature Through Serendipitous Encounters with Mud 103
Tracy Ann Hayes

Chapter 6 – 'No Badge Required': A Bucket School Approach to Support Teaching and Learning in the Outdoors 121
Louise Hawxwell and Nicky Bolton

PART 3: CONTINUING THE JOURNEY OF PLACE-RESPONSIVE PEDAGOGY IN OUTDOOR LEARNING

Chapter 7 – The Next Generation of Learning Outside: Fostering Place-responsive Pedagogy in Initial Teacher Education 141
Lucy Sors, Jen Huntsley and Stephanie Jach

Chapter 8 – Continuing the Journey of Place-responsive Pedagogy in Outdoor Learning 161
Ruth Unsworth and Lucy Sors

References 167

Index 185

List of Figures and Table

Fig. 0.1.	Take Five Exercise.	13
Fig. 1.1.	Spatial and Temporal Experiences of Place.	20
Fig. 1.2.	Habitus as Method: Internal Components and Field (Akram, 2023, p. 206).	27
Fig. 3.1.	Adaptive Critical Pedagogy.	64
Fig. 3.2.	Holistic Assessment in Outdoor Learning.	68
Fig. 4.1.	A Topology of a School 'forest' as Educational Place.	93
Fig. 6.1.	Bucket School in Action.	132
Fig. 6.2.	Different Learning and Teaching Activities Can Be Carried Out in Bucket School in all Weathers.	134
Fig. 6.3.	Bucket School in Uganda.	136
Fig. 7.1.	Re-conceptualised Model of Korthagen et al.'s *Three Levels of Changing Teacher Behaviour*.	145
Fig. 7.2.	'Level reduction' Mindmap of the OL Module.	151
Table 3.1.	Questions to Support Reflection and Dialogue Around Safety and Belonging.	76

About the Editors

Lucy Sors is a Senior Lecturer and Inclusion Lead in initial teacher education (ITE) at York St John University. She teaches across ITE programmes specialising in outdoor learning (OL), SEND and inclusion, and languages. Lucy has worked as Special Educational Needs and Disabilities Coordinator (SENDCo), school leader, teacher and researcher in primary schools in Scotland, Northeast England, France and Morocco. Prior to teaching, she worked for organisations supporting children, young people and adults with additional support needs in a range of settings including outdoor education and play-based learning. Her research seeks to include multiple 'voices' to inform creative, participatory and inclusive pedagogies in education, stemming from her academic background in social anthropology and development and her work supporting diverse children, young people and their families.

Ruth Unsworth is a Lecturer in Education Studies at the University of Glasgow. Since 2003, Ruth has dedicated her career to exploring education and its practices. Ruth has taught in English state and independent schools and in international schools in Italy and Japan. As well as teaching and leading in primary education, Ruth offers education consultancy, focusing on place-based pedagogy and creative approaches to education. After recently working as Senior Lecturer in ITE, Ruth currently holds a research and teaching post at the University of Glasgow. Her research and publications include new materialist and psychoanalytic perspectives of educational practices exploring the role of plurality, conversation and place in education. She is part of the organising committee for the annual Oxford Ethnography and Education Conference and a member of the International Teacher Education Research Collective (ITERC).

About the Contributors

Nicky Bolton is Headteacher at Tattenhall Park Primary School. She has been a primary school teacher for 30 years and was delighted to meet Louise whilst lecturing at Edge Hill University. As a passionate advocate of OL, Bucket School evolved as a consequence of her research into *nature capital* – the knowledge and experiences of the outdoors gained during children's formative years. She is a Primary Science Teaching Trust Fellow and currently coordinates environmental school initiatives between the UK and Uganda.

Louise Hawxwell is a Lecturer in primary teacher education at Moray House School of Education and Sport, University of Edinburgh. She has worked in ITE since 2011, both in England and in Scotland. Prior to this, she was a primary school teacher for 12 years, teaching across the primary age range. She is passionate about the outdoors and in supporting teachers and student teachers in taking learning outside in creative ways.

Tracy Ann Hayes is Associate Dean (Research and Innovation) in the School of Education at Plymouth Marjon University. With a PhD in Transdisciplinary Research in Outdoor Studies awarded by Lancaster University for research into young people's relationship with the natural environment, she embraces transdisciplinary methodologies that utilise creative and narrative approaches to research nature, OL and play, youth work, community development and informal learning. Publications include: chapter author in von Benzon, N., Holton, M., Wilkinson et al., S. (2021). *Creative methods for human geographers*; chapter author in Barker, J. & Wainwright, E. (section eds.). In J. Parsons and A. Chappell (Eds.).

(2020). *The Palgrave MacMillan handbook of auto/biography*; and lead editor and chapter author in Hayes, T. A., Edlmann, T., & Brown, L. (2019). *Storytelling: Global perspectives on narrative*. In 2018, she was awarded the Anna Craft Creativities in Education Prize by BERA Creativities in Education.

Jen Huntsley is a Senior Lecturer in ITE at York St John University, specialising in primary English, design and technology, history and OL. Her research is centred on the development of student teachers' learning within universities and HEIs and how this influences their future practice. She has developed novel methodologies in the field of enterprise education research, recently published in Fayolle, A., Le Pontois, S., & Pelly, D. M., (eds.). (2024). *Big questions and great answers in entrepreneurship research* (co-authored with Dr. Catherine Brentnall). Previously, she has worked in primary school leadership roles, both in the UK and in Thailand. She is an advocate of learning through play, creativity and the outdoors and enjoys sharing these passions with her young family.

Stephanie Jach is a Lecturer in ITE at York St John University. She teaches across ITE specialising in history, geography, citizenship and OL. She taught in primary schools in Yorkshire and the North East in England and led primary history and geography before moving into ITE. She is passionate about social justice in education. Before teaching, she worked for an international development charity supporting education projects in the Global South. Her master's degree research in Development Anthropology investigated the impact of volunteers on education projects in Tanzania. As well as OL, her current research focusses on citizenship education using participatory action research.

Louise Whitfield is a Senior Lecturer and Programme Lead in ITE at York St John University. She specialises in inclusion and early years (EY) education and leads on personal, social, health, and economic (PSHE) education in ITE. With a background in primary teaching, she has taught across several different areas in England and has held responsibilities such as key stage leader. Much of her research stems from her interest in EY education or from her role as Early Career Teacher (ECT) Lead. Her doctoral thesis focussed on ECT identity and how this is navigated against the current educational policy context. This lens also extends to looking at a range of pedagogies to enable inclusive practice.

Foreword

In an age marked by increasing disconnection from the natural world, the urgent need for holistic, place-responsive outdoor learning (OL) has never been more apparent. *The BERA Guide to Outdoor Learning: Place-responsive Pedagogy in Educational Research and Practice* arrives as a must-read for educators, researchers, and practitioners, offering a visionary framework to reimagine education in ways that nurture both individuals and the planet. This book is not merely an academic text; it is an invitation to rekindle our relationships with place, self, and community through the transformative power of OL. This book is a most welcome, timely, and transformative text that is highly recommended.

This collection, meticulously edited by Lucy Sors and Ruth Unsworth, is a timely response to pressing societal, environmental, and educational challenges. Rooted in the foundational concept of place-responsive pedagogy, the book breaks traditional educational boundaries. It speaks directly to educators navigating the post-pandemic era, struggling with the intensified pressures of curriculum delivery and neoliberal performance metrics. By grounding its insights in a dynamic interplay of theory, practice, and lived experience, this book equips readers to rise above these controls and imagine new, inclusive possibilities for teaching and learning.

Central to the book is the recognition that OL holds unrivalled potential to address critical global concerns, including mental health crises, environmental degradation, and social inequities. The authors make a compelling case for OL as a means of fostering resilience, creativity, and a sense of belonging in young people. Highlighting the joy and well-being that nature can bring, as evidenced by the surveys from Natural England, the book champions OL not only as an educational tool but as a pathway to reconnection with our shared environment. Structured thoughtfully, *The BERA Guide to Outdoor Learning: Place-responsive Pedagogy in Educational*

Research and Practice weaves together theoretical insights and practical applications. Early chapters establish a robust conceptual foundation, inviting readers to critically examine the role of place in education. Through discussions on decolonising OL, inclusive practice, and child-centred learning, the book challenges our cultural norms, urging educators to adopt responsive approaches that honour diverse identities and experiences. Subsequent chapters illustrate these ideas in action, drawing on rich empirical examples such as Forest Schools, 'Bucket Schools', and playful explorations of 'mudfulness'. These case studies bring the theoretical concepts to life, demonstrating the transformative power of OL across different settings.

What sets this book apart is its emphasis on inclusivity and adaptability. By addressing OL beyond the early years and exploring diverse environments, from urban landscapes to virtual spaces, it expands the field of OL horizons. The authors' call for equitable access ensures that all children, regardless of background or ability, can benefit from the profound learning opportunities that outdoor experiences can provide. As the final chapters turn their focus to Initial Teacher Education (ITE), the text highlights the importance of empowering the next generation of educators. Through innovative approaches to ITE, the authors outline a path towards a future where OL is not a peripheral activity but a central pillar of education.

The BERA Guide to Outdoor Learning: Place-responsive Pedagogy in Educational Research and Practice is a celebration of possibility. It urges readers to pause, reflect and reimagine what education could be when it embraces the interconnectedness of place, people and purpose. By championing a responsive, holistic and inclusive vision of OL, this book offers a much-needed antidote to the challenges of contemporary education. It is an essential read for anyone committed to cultivating meaningful, world-centred pedagogies and nurturing a generation of learners prepared to thrive in and care for a rapidly changing world. This book resonates strongly with me and the direction of our theory and practice in contemporary OL. Read this book!

– Mark Leather
**Associate Professor of Education
School of Education
Plymouth Marjon University**

Acknowledgements

This book has been underpinned by so many experiences, in so many places, with so many people. We are grateful for every conversation, experience, and rabbit hole we have fallen into with our patient and supportive colleagues, friends, and family.

Our thanks and congratulations firstly go to our contributing authors to this book. Their commitment to OL and inspirational guidance has greatly influenced this volume. We thank Tracy Hayes, Louise Hawxwell, and Mark Leather for encouraging us to pursue place-responsive pedagogy as an important area of focus in OL. For continuing passion and dedication to developing OL in schools, we thank Nicky Bolton. Our co-authors, friends and colleagues Louise Whitfield, Jen Huntsley, and Steph Jach have tirelessly championed this project, not least through their innovative contributions, but also through their daily practices as teacher–educators, pushing the boundaries of what is possible in ITE. We know you have enjoyed this journey as much as we have!

Special thanks are given to the following people for offering their generous and invaluable critiques, suggestions and proofreading on individual chapters:

Beth Reed

Sarah Trussler

Tom Dobson

We also thank pupils, students and peers we have worked with over the years for their inspiring engagement and participation in OL.

Finally, to our children, Georgie, Margot, and Rose, who continually surprise us through their creative ways of connecting to places. We delight in their muddy escapades that inspire us daily. This book is dedicated to them.

Introduction: Encountering Ideas of Place in Outdoor Learning

Lucy Sors[a] and Ruth Unsworth[b]
[a]York St John University, UK
[b]University of Glasgow, UK

A Slow Start

Our principal aim in this book is to offer a contribution to the field of outdoor learning (OL) in education research and practice, explored within a framework of place-responsive pedagogy. We explore how approaches to place can help us understand what it means to take education outdoors, and how most effectively to 'do' it. The verb 'do' may immediately call the reader into action, to try to seek a conclusion, or to focus on *what* to 'do'. However, if we allow ourselves to 'pause for more than a fleeting moment' (Payne & Wattchow, 2009, p. 16), we can escape from the restrictions of time, tuning in to our interests and motivations to engage more deeply with experiences in whatever role we are assuming at that moment. Embracing *slow* enables adoption of a patient, deliberate approach to research, theory and practice, which we rarely afford ourselves amongst contemporary pressures and busy-ness (Clark, 2021). By engaging with theoretical and practical examples of OL throughout this book, we aim to journey to places, communities and ecosystems (Beames et al., 2024), to prompt consideration of place-responsive pedagogy. Threads interwoven throughout these chapters are part of a broad pedagogical exploration of OL. We explore the artistry of outdoor educational practice informed by practice, dialogue, research and critical consideration.

This book is first and foremost rooted in experience. We recognise our intersecting identities as researchers, practitioners, teachers, teacher–educators, students and parents. Contributing authors have stepped inside and outside of each of these roles, engaging in OL in different directions and different places. In a pivotal conversation within the BERA Special Interest Group (SIG) 'Nature, Outdoor Learning and Play', we reflected on positives and conflicts within our encounters of education outside classrooms. What became clear is a conviction we all share: that children should be spending more time outdoors and that experiences outdoors should provide opportunities for holistic learning, playful exploration and reconnection. Reconnection to self, others and the world we find ourselves in. It is from this starting point that we begin our collective writing journey. We invite our readers to spend time designing their own pedagogical canvas on this reflexive journey into OL.

Entering the Field of OL

Let us start by situating ourselves within the metaphorical field of OL. Upon entering the field, we find a patchwork of disciplines and terms, each defining itself around different notions of 'subject', 'content', 'method' and 'practice' (Roberts, 2018). The multifaceted nature of OL reflects its interdisciplinary background: its benefits, conflicts and challenges have been discussed in the fields of geography, anthropology, health and psychology. Within education research, interest in OL has grown, recognising benefits to mental health and well-being, physical wellness, cultural and cognitive development, as well as supporting growing momentum in sustainability and environmental education.

Wide-ranging definitions surround teaching and learning that take place outside of traditional education settings such as classrooms. The terms *outdoor education* and *outdoor learning*, for example, are often used interchangeably. However, the former is weighted towards outdoor and adventurous activities within the Physical Education curriculum (Sanderud et al., 2021), and criticised for its tendency to conflate different forms of 'education outside' under one term (Brookes, 2002). Another term 'learning outside the classroom' (LOTC), as coined by the DfES in 2006 through the LOTC Manifesto, suggests that all children should access 'the world beyond the classroom' by teaching curriculum subjects outside with an emphasis on experiential learning: 'Learning outside the classroom is about raising achievement through an organised, powerful approach to learning in which direct experience is of prime importance' (DfES, 2006, p. 3). This is problematic in that 'raising achievement' indicates a mere continuation of narrowed outcomes valued in schooling that emphasises curriculum over encountering the world (Waite & Pratt, 2017). More recently, Beames et al. (2024) have moved beyond LOTC, with the idea of OL *across* and *beyond* the curriculum, conceptualised as pedagogy which, whilst teaching intended learning outcomes, remains open to the value of the *unintended* (Beames et al., 2024, p. 2). Continuing to position OL pedagogy in relation to 'learning outcomes' could negate the value of learning outdoors as an *evolving* and *responsive* experience, to do with development of the self and one's understanding of the world. That said, Beames et al.'s definition develops a vision with much broader 'outcomes':

> Outdoor learning is an educational process *that allows a learner to develop knowledge, skills, attitudes, and behaviours through direct engagement with outdoor environments, and which provides the learner with a range of personal, educational, and social benefits, which may have wider value for society and the planet* (Beames et al., 2024, p. 2).

This connected, holistic understanding of OL incorporates a range of principles and approaches, which may support formal, informal or alternative curricula (Beames et al., 2024, p. 28) and/or step *outside* of organised curriculum teaching. Such plurality opens conversation around the value of the 'otherness' of education; for example, open-ended encounters with the world and the importance of unintended learning alongside planned curriculum outcomes. OL involves meeting with, discussion about and experience of dynamic entities; it involves being present in (or thinking about) the things, ideas and people encountered. It encompasses implicit skills, approaches and 'hidden' curriculum outcomes that will result from interactions in different places. It is around this potentiality of an educational *process in places* that we direct our readers' focus.

Essentially, OL, in this book, denotes a holistic pedagogy that centres teaching and learning '*in*, *about*, and *for* the outdoors' (Donaldson & Donaldson, 1958, p. 17, our emphasis). OL simultaneously signifies places to teach and learn *in*, a focus to teach and learn *about*, and an approach that advocates *for* the world outside of policy-curated classrooms. We use the term to provide emphasis on the multifarious dynamic and messy processes of coming to know, understand and be able to interact with the world, the self and others, through experiences. Our use of 'outdoor learning' also seeks to exit the 'learnification' trend in education discourse, practice and research; a trend which over(t)ly focusses attention on learners in relation to defined outcomes and goals, rather than on *teaching* that moves students' thought and action forwards (Biesta, 2010; Biesta, 2023). We reimagine and resituate 'learning' as a consequence of 'teaching' – refocussing the purpose of education as supporting children to connect themselves, others and the world in a care-full, play-full, responsive manner. This entails teachers' consideration and deployment of the nature, character and potential of learning *in, about and for* place(s).

We see OL as a key pedagogical approach in that 'education has to take place in the *here and now*' (Biesta, 2021, p. 11); it has the power to enliven and activate students' awareness *of* the here and now. We adopt a place-responsive approach to OL, based on the understanding that it can 'take place' anywhere. Teaching and learning is situated in *places*: a presentness in space-time that is entangled with sociocultural histories, long-established ways of being and knowing, and spaces of possibility that open through place-based encounters. This vision for OL is inherently *responsive*, adapting to changing contexts, demands and pressures in both local and global contexts. We therefore underpin our discussion of OL with place-responsiveness to consider *connections* between physical situations, *processes* of encounter and *reflections* on experience. This concerns *what, where* and *how* we teach and learn but also *why* we teach what we teach and learn what we learn (Waite & Pratt, 2017).

The Urgency of OL

The history and evolution of OL has been previously explored (see, e.g. Oglivie, 2013), and we do not wish to replicate this here. Instead, we focus on the urgency of OL in the *here* and *now*. OL is of particular importance in current educational landscapes in western contexts where neoliberal post-pandemic social trends place great emphasis on 'delivery' of, and 'catch-up' within, prioritised national curriculum subjects. In England, as in many countries, time outside for children is in decline, both at home and at school (Baines & Blatchford, 2019). We know from recent national surveys conducted with children and young people (CYP), that being in nature has a positive impact on their emotional and cognitive well-being. However, we also know that two-thirds of children are not provided with opportunities to do activities or lessons outside at school aside from PE and that nearly half of CYP surveyed did not feel a 'high' connection to nature (Natural England's Children's People and Nature Survey for England, 2023). Decline in active experience of natural places and disconnection to the world are associated with a real risk that 'the next generation of UK adults will be the least healthy in living memory' (D'Souza, quoted by the Children's Alliance, 2021, n.p.). Mental and physical health crises overwhelm public services and create extreme challenges to educational provision and inclusion (DfE, 2023). Contemporary OL research engaged with throughout this book builds on the multiple benefits of being outside to explore how education may provide opportunities to participate in authentic, memorable and connected learning experiences. This is an inherently *responsive* approach, which seeks to actively address social, environmental and historical inequalities through critical engagement with *world-self-others* encounters. Experiences in OL are planned to transcend typical educational settings, challenge prescribed educational agendas and reconnect humans to the world. (Mannion & Lynch, 2016; Muñoz, 2009).

Present and future uncertainties surrounding climate change and global conflict have reawakened conversations around the types of experiences and skills that CYP need throughout (and outside of) formal education. There is a disconnect between national curricula and research/profession-led 'movements' in this regard. Despite the pressures of contemporary society and global threats to human existence and individual well-being, educators are asked to 'forget' or 'ignore' wider world issues in the drive to deliver a prescribed educational agenda (Biesta, 2021). Simultaneously, the importance of transferable skills has been established, such as problem-solving, adaptability, critical and innovative thinking and intra/interpersonal skills for future-proofing the next generation in a world of constant change (UNESCO, 2016).

Advocates of OL recognise its ability to introduce responsiveness, risk and challenge; to build resilience and resourcefulness in varying contexts (Beames et al, 2024). A quiet rebellion is mounting against mainstream neoliberalist ideologies of performativity, to offer alternative visions such as 'world-centred education' (Biesta, 2021) and education that prioritises connectivism, learner agency and adaptability to change. However, whilst these are important ideas, they currently remain mainly abstracted; detached from the contexts and realities in which they could lend value. In this book, we seek to ground the important elements of contemporary educational thinking that can inform curriculum design and implementation. Chapters make suggestions around practice that can build connections, support teacher and learner agency and build robust approaches to adaptability. We aim to promote criticality by questionning assumptions about education, 'progress', society and culture. Thus, the case is made for place-responsive learning within the development of educational practice that will foster inclusion, individual agency and personal and societal responsibility to the world, ourselves, and others. We situate these considerations physically, temporally and as lived experience in an OL context. In this way, we develop a response to world-centred education and related philosophy, that 'entails an intervention at the level of educational practice' (Biesta, 2025, p.536). This involves raising practitioner awareness of *place*, (and encounters in and with places), and its role in forging world-self-other connections.

Towards Place-responsive Pedagogy in OL

Whilst it is important to recognise the diversity of discourse and growing significance of the field of OL, it is useful to find a perspective to speak to this diversity amongst a scarcity of research that pays attention to its theoretical foundations (Hawxwell et al., 2019). There are difficulties in any endeavour to theoretically unify diverse practices: there is unlikely to be a single definition of OL that suits the variegated forms of experiences which happen outdoors. Arguing for such a definition might be restrictive or reductive to the opportunities presented by OL and something of a conceptual minefield. Instead, we present a question that runs throughout this book: how might considerations of *place* in relation to *education* be useful to OL?

It is perhaps useful to first consider the large terms of education and place. Through an education-focussed research community, the editors of this book found themselves united by discussions of 'what is education?'. Our experiences teaching and studying abroad, interests in socio-cultural understandings of place, academic histories rooted in social anthropology and a shared passion for travel and the outdoors; this is what informed our reading of education. For us, education is fundamentally a belief in a purposeful, responsive act which has transformative power to guide a social 'becoming': a leading of attention *towards* becoming in life, in the world and with others (Ingold, 2018). Different worlds demand and instruct different encounters and different pedagogical responses. This demands a multi-versal approach within the social principles of 'world-centred education'; which 'world' are we seeking for our children to 'meet'? This is not a 'one-catch-all' standardised model of education; it needs to be *responsive* to people, places and times and implement mindful inclusion. It is an education that seeks to address barriers to the world and open opportunities to engage with it.

Returning to the *process* of education, this visualises teaching as a variety of encounters between people, materials, ideas, memories, wishes, etc., which intricately entangle as a tapestry of *becoming*. Having engaged in ethnographic enquiry, immersing ourselves in various 'fields', we view the tapestry of education (and of this book) as woven by history, philosophy, anthropology, politics, psychology, language, art, sociology and geography … in short, informed by interdisciplinary in-world exchange. Culture, belonging and human behaviour lie at its heart, pivoting around the 'here and now' of place. We firmly believe in foregrounding and acknowledging lived experience in and of education, and the necessity of complicating what may at first seem quite simple ideas: for example, the notion of where learning takes place and its relation to educational intentions.

Whilst there are many aspects of our philosophy of education which we could focus on, this book takes up and interrogates *place* through the voices of contributing authors who, despite differences in our experiences, all relate to a shared aim: the desire to disseminate practice and research around the value of place-responsive pedagogy in OL. Learning from our own ventures into the outdoors as educators, researchers and in our personal lives, we understand place-responsive pedagogy as a valuable approach to support, improve and restore relationships between humans and the world (Mannion & Lynch, 2016). We delve deeper into notions of place in Chapter 1; however, broadly speaking, we see place as a continuum, made not only of material physicality, but also of ideas of place, of cultural signification and practices that must be considered in facilitating a relationship with the environment. An indoors/outdoors binary is, therefore, unhelpful. Instead, a shift towards '*ideas* of place in education' (Rawlings Smith & Pike, 2024, our emphasis) supports a broader vision for place in OL. Place-responsive learning in, about and for the outdoors can take place outdoors or indoors: in nature or urban environments, indoors interacting with outdoor artefacts, in transient, fixed or fluid places, in virtual spaces or imaginative places (Beames et al., 2024). Place-responsive pedagogy is focussed on how teaching (as the deliberate enactment of an educational philosophy) may facilitate experiential connections, through curation of place-based responses and sensory experiences, support critical knowledge of a place's historical and cultural space-time, and build relationships.

In our explorations of place-responsive pedagogy in OL, we build from an insightful collected volume *Encountering Ideas of Place in Education* (Rawlings Smith & Pike, 2024), which explores place-based approaches in different research contexts and studies. We offer place-responsiveness as a way of educators preparing for the wide range of inextricable and unpredictable educational outcomes resulting from encounters with place. Preparing in this sense is about getting ready to encourage, and remain open to, the endless possibilities of place-response, mediated by action, relationships and activity that may be planned, or unplanned, in various contexts. This book supports a conscious move to critically and creatively explore the value of place-based experiences as responsive, generative and transformative learning processes resulting from direct interactions within authentic environments.

Central to the philosophy underpinning this book is a commitment to pursuing equal and uninhibited access to OL for *all*. This means enacting practice that enables every individual full and rich encounters with a full range of places and experiences; educational action that supports CYP to interact with different places in different ways and to build their own relationships with self, others and the world. This book aims to celebrate experiences in the outdoors through examples of how 'primacy of place' (Mannion & Lynch, 2016) can support outcomes (however these are construed), relationships, agency, well-being and creativity. This involves critical confrontation of difficult truths around places tackling issues such as access, exclusion, and social injustices; implicit and explicit messages that informs a *'critical pedagogy of place'* (Gruenewald, 2003). Contributing authors advocate for an inherently inclusive educational approach, which addresses barriers to participation, and also seeks to develop repair and restitution of relationships with places. We focus a conversation towards how OL can respond to 'what is the world asking of us' (Biesta, 2025), by which CYP can engage in playful communion with the world to benefit the environment, themselves and their communities. This book extends the typical focus in OL literature to beyond the Early Years and beyond 'the outside'; considering OL more generally and as applicable to all ages, backgrounds, educational needs and stages of education, in different places. The theories and approaches presented are easily adapted to support all CYP in establishing and maintaining *world-self-other* connections, in various 'situative' (in relation to a specific situation) encounters.

Chapter Introductions

The book is organised in three parts. In Part One, we explore the theoretical underpinnings of place-responsive pedagogy and consider theory as practice. In Chapter 1, Lucy Sors introduces the reader to place-responsive pedagogy, developing a theoretical basis and considering its practical implications for planning educational encounters through OL. In Chapter 2, Lucy Sors and Louise Whitfield discuss decolonising approaches to OL and how practitioners may develop connectedness through place-responsive pedagogy in education beyond the Early Years. In Chapter 3, Lucy Sors provides an essential chapter for all practitioners planning to put the ideas of this book into practice. This chapter focusses on inclusive and holistic practice in place-responsive OL, exploring agency, accessibility and participation.

Part Two turns to empirical examples of place-responsive pedagogy in action. In Chapter 4, Ruth Unsworth analyses ethnographic research in a primary phase Forest School through a social topological lens, considering how social topology can help teachers to plan for meaningful place connection. Next, Tracy Ann Hayes explores her study of nature connection with adolescents through mud, highlighting a need for kindness, playfulness and 'mudfulness' in developing positive relationships with nature. In Chapter 6, Louise Hawxwell and Nicky Bolton draw on empirical examples of 'Bucket School' both in Primary Education and in Teacher Education to challenge the notion of requiring a qualification to teach outdoors.

The final part to this book presents the reader with reflections on the future of place-responsive pedagogy in OL. Chapter 7 considers the next generation of learning outside by exploring approaches to fostering place-responsive pedagogy in ITE. In this chapter, Lucy Sors, Jen Hunstley and Stephanie Jach demonstrate how experiential learning plays an important role in developing teachers who are confident in taking learning to places beyond the classroom. Chapter 8 considers how to continue the journey of place-responsive pedagogy in OL, returning to the importance of open-endedness of place connection, resistance of over-prescription of the educational experience, and the value of taking our time to exist in the places we encounter.

This book explores how practitioners can and should, in the words of Mark Leather during a BERA SIG, 'push at the door so it opens' to support world-self-other connections, emerging through relationships formed in interactions with place. As editors, we hope that our readers find the theoretical considerations, as well as interesting examples of theory in practice, a useful starting point for their own endeavours in OL.

In reflection upon this introduction, we offer for consideration the following questions. Not as rhetorical points, but for the reader to consider as they develop their own relationship to this book:

- *How can OL support us to address educational, social, environmental and wider world issues?*
- *How can OL support ideas around connection, inclusion, agency and relationships within and to the world?*
- *How have rapid technological expansion and teaching methods that prioritise paper- or screen-based learning impacted on our experience of the world?*
- *What sort of relationship does the next generation have with the outdoors and therefore what value do they place on its protection?*
- *How can OL support children and young people to encounter and 'meet' the world?*
- *How can teachers and researchers be responsive to places in planning OL pedagogy?*

A Pause for Connection

Lucy Sors
York St John University, UK

We invite the reader to pause and consider their own journey to *here* and *now* by engaging in an exercise in spatial and temporal reflection. Mindful approaches support self-regulation and greater sensitivity to our environment. Through a process of 'grounding' ourselves, we can experience deeper connection, and increase our sense of involvement in a place, encounter or moment. Short, therapeutic intervention activities designed to support body awareness are an effective technique to use with a variety of learners in OL, to bring them into the *here-and-now* and to support connections to place.

Take a moment to reflect and connect to the place you are in at this present moment. Then, 'take five' by engaging with the process outlined in Fig 0.1. As you move through each step in Fig. 0.1, draw awareness to your senses and bodily sensations.

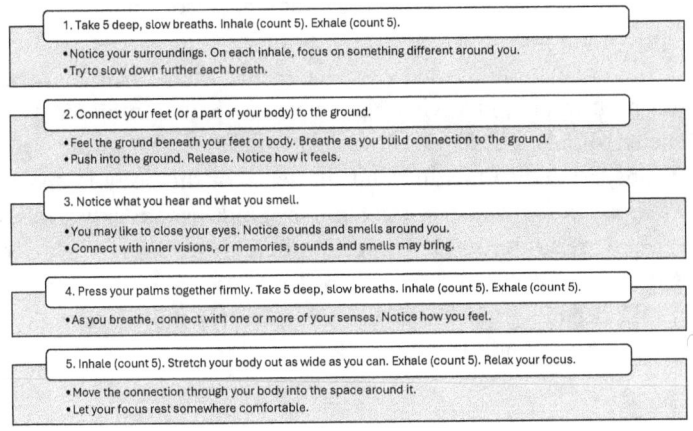

Fig. 0.1. Take Five Exercise.

Once 'grounded', we can begin an exercise in spatial and temporal reflection to establish deeper connections to place. 'Take five' might be a useful starting point to use 'live' with individuals in an outdoor space, or, to generate a mental image of place, evoking memories and imagination (see Chapter 1, Fig. 1.1). Connections to place – physical, metaphysical, psychological, and emotional – establish an essential foundation to situated experiences. From here, *mindful place-based education* (Deringer, 2017) can open doors into critical pedagogies of place (Gruenewald, 2003), and deepen experiences of world-self-others connections. All places have a past, present and future (Beames et al. 2024, p.68), and do not have to be explicitly situated in the moment to be experienced. Connections to place can be imagined, envisaged or remembered. Read the below prompts and 'take' yourself to a place in your mind:

- *Where are you drawn to? What can you hear/see/smell? How does it make you feel?* (**Present**)
- *What are your memories of that place? What did you do?* (**Past**)
- *What might happen there? How might it change?* (**Future**)

These questions, which can be adapted according to setting, support a structured routine to connect with a space, based on the understanding that experience of place is socio-cultural and multimodal, involving all the senses. Sights intersect with smells, sounds and tastes. Movement and touch bring other sensations, related to tactility and the sense of the body in space. '*Phenomenological deconstruction*' reminds us that experiences of place are subjective, corporeal and highly personal (Payne & Wattchow, 2009). Therefore, in order to gain a *'sense of place'* in OL, pedagogy must account and plan for multisensoriality, memory and mindfulness.

PART 1

Theorising Place-responsive Pedagogy in Outdoor Learning

CHAPTER 1

Place-responsive Pedagogy in Outdoor Learning

Lucy Sors
York St John University, UK

ABSTRACT

This chapter introduces the reader to place-responsive pedagogy within outdoor learning (OL). Place is conceptualised around ideas of connection, supporting readers to reconsider and deepen understanding around this term. A socio-cultural perspective of place intensifies the notion of place-responsive pedagogy and supports teachers' planning for outdoor experiences. Readers are invited to reflect on their own experiences of place in order to position themselves within a place-responsive pedagogical philosophy.

Introduction

In this first chapter, place-responsive pedagogy is situated at the heart of practice in OL. *Place* is conceptualised differently within and across a variety of disciplines. This chapter unites theories developed in education, sociology, psychology, and social anthropology to inform theory and pedagogy around place-centred OL. Place cannot be reduced to a single definition; it has ethereal qualities which echo memory, interaction and emotion, which fit uneasily alongside capitalist performativity and marketisation. Such complications have led to contention of *place*, underpinning a trend amongst contemporary authors to conceptualise place as measurable components: geographic 'space' (physical dimensions and boundaries of sites) and chronological 'time' (tracking changes over time) (Casey, 1997). Criticisms of this approach centre around space and/or time confining cultural and social activity to physical and temporal boundaries; instead, place extends beyond geographic sites and moments-in-time (Appadurai, 1988; Rawlings Smith & Pike, 2024; Unsworth, 2024). Place-*responsive* pedagogy unshackles from restrictive definitions to focus on the facilitation of interactions between self and place and others in different spaces, applying different concepts of time. This approach moves beyond measurable components and outcomes to centre on relationships and connection.

Conceptualising Place and Place Connection

Pedagogy is, essentially, *place-based* (Mannion & Lynch, 2016; Wattchow & Brown, 2011). If we are to educate in places (which of course, we do, whether indoors, outdoors, online etc.), we must consider the complex pre-existing and ongoing sociomaterial activity that is the continuous (re)construction of place, of place connection and pedagogy within places. Decisions around practice are situated within educational policy-scapes and ecosystems – therefore pedagogy *responds* to place. Put simply, OL is 'using the local environment as a starting point to teach concepts' (Sobel, 2004, p. 7). This idea is not novel. From the early 20th century, Dewey (1938) argued for progressive education which contextualised learning in the real world. This challenged abstract ideas around 'education of the world', delivered through detached curricula confined to classrooms. A place-responsive pedagogical approach situates education as *lived experience*, explored through a dynamic and transformative learning process. This focusses on evolving interactions between people and places, and progressive learning about how to solve problems expanding from the 'local' to places more distant and removed (Sobel, 2004).

Evolving from Dewey's conceptualisation of education as a 'process of living', experiential learning engages in a process of *doing*. Powerful connections are, therefore, established through experiences *in* places. As a form of education, place-responsive pedagogy does not view the world as a 'static reality' but rather as 'dynamic, where students are challenged to construct their own meanings and teachers strive to make education engaging and empowering. (...) [It is a] powerful tool that assists educators in reducing placelessness and the decontextualization [sic] embedded in standardized [sic] curricula' (Deringer et al., 2020, p. 121).

Places are full of history in the form of collective and individualised memory (which sometimes agrees, sometimes conflicts) as constituent parts of what we know as 'culture' and 'society'. Two pivotal concepts developed by Pierre Bourdieu (1930–2002) interrogate a socio-cultural understanding of place: *habitus* and *doxa*. These key ideas draw attention to the relationship between diverse educational intentions and drive the kind of places we choose as the site of educational experience. A *place of pedagogy* (where pedagogy is situated), is, therefore, not just a physical, material site, but also full of previous and ongoing social activity and assignations of meaning and affect: a space of social experience. Places are translated through *habitus* (how individuals perceive and respond to the social world around them) and individual principles intermingle with values that enter the local from *doxa* (a set of unquestioned taken-for-granted beliefs about the world). *Habitus* is informed through memories of (1) the associations of people, things, language and ideals that are impacted by affective dominance in terms of what is valued or rejected *doxa* in social groups and (2) *interplace relationality* in terms of how places relate to other places.

Relationships with places are, thus, both founded upon, and continuations of socio-material memory, or projection – a sort of 'longing' between past and future which creates the present (Ingold, 2018). A key aspect of place-responsive pedagogy is therefore understanding different histories of places, including conflicting values, access and actions: 'places are full of beauty and wonder, but they are also framed by economic, systemic, and historical factors, including power differences, that determine people's life opportunities' (Beames et al., 2024, p.65). This results in a collective communing with or individual rejection of culture and material–human emotional and cognitive associations. Children have already established relationships with the world by the time they reach the place of pedagogy. In their interactions in places (both planned for and unplanned), they come to each experience as (accepted/

rebellious) part of the complex web of sociomateriality and socioculturality of that place. They are a part of the place, not separate from it: place and people are simultaneously interrelated. However, each individual will experience different feelings and responses in different places, given socio-cultural realties: included/excluded, connected/disconnected, accepted/rejected. Our prime consideration for OL should be what relationships are *already in place* and how to build on, challenge or evolve these relationships.

'Place' must be explored in its complexity, rather than simplified, to grasp it, and this must first be tackled before we can set about exploring place within OL. Relationships between people and place, and what happens within that place, are built through encounters which transcend the immediate space and time.

Place connection is beyond the present and involves interaction between different temporal and spatial planes. This is represented in Fig. 1.1.

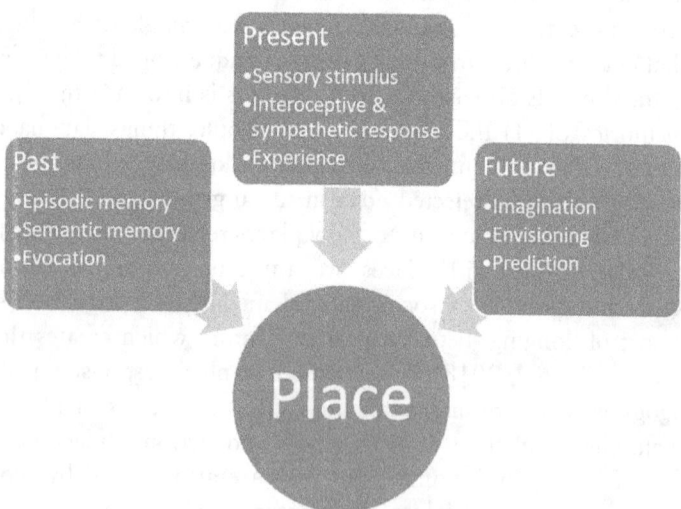

Fig. 1.1. Spatial and Temporal Experiences of Place.

Individual responses are activated by a range of factors that might be intangible or difficult to describe to others. The fields of psychology and neuroscience can inform what is happening as our brain responds to the stimulus of any given experience in the present, which triggers interoceptive and sympathetic responses. The concept of 'crossmodal imagery' indicates that mental imagery can occur in any sensory plane (Spence & Deroy, 2013, p. 157) and can result from objects, experiences and places which have been interacted with through another sensory modality (Deroy, 2020, p. 276). Beyond the 'live' experience of a place, mental imagery spans across the senses and transcends space and time, as we switch between past and present encounters. We access, form and retrieve the temporal–spatial details from different memories of specific past events; our *episodic memory* (Tulving, 1972). This can be triggered by a place, object, or sensory experience, drawing on past experiences and creating meaning – or, as Tulving terms it, a 'mental thesaurus': our *semantic memory* (Tulving, 1972, p. 386). Below, a vignette of a personal experience illustrates connections between episodic and semantic memory:

> *When I see fallen trees with one large branch sticking upright, I remember episodes from my childhood that played out on a similar tree. The fallen tree was precariously perched on a hillside path at the middle-point of a walk in Swaledale and was the key motivator to conquer the drag up the hill for me and my sister. Picnics on the tree were a welcome break to the hilly walk, and an escape from any present concerns. Upon connecting with this memory, my senses are activated. The tree is seemingly unchanged over time. I can smell the distinct scent of the Yorkshire Dales; the sheep, the grass, the rotting wood. The taste of satsumas is tangible – a food we habitually ate on our tree den. I hear birds, soft baaing of sheep and the breeze whispering through the wood. The air feels chilled on my face. The smooth tree provides satisfying sensory feedback as I slide along its weather-beaten, bleached trunk. I remember the sense of almost falling but mainly balancing; a sense of precarious risk as I climbed up the unstable branches. This feeling is reactivated nowadays, as I watch my own children scale other fallen trees.*

This vignette demonstrates an episodic memory that is intrinsically linked to the stimulus of the image: the fallen tree.

A general understanding of the world [semantic memory], and my connection to it, is enriched by this episode, alongside others, as my brain builds knowledge and meaning. In the present, interoceptive and sympathetic responses were stimulated by the experience of being in a fallen tree place. Experience is reproduced in the brain, involving a feat of imagination which relies on sensorial engagement and *connection to place*. The brain recalls 'cross-modal' imagery from the site of experience resulting from repeated interactions deeply rooted within the senses (Spence & Deroy, 2013).

Moving beyond memories – from the past, through the present and to imagine the future – we recombine episodic, semantic and sensory memories to create new simulations of what *could* happen based on our informed predictions. Possibilities unfurl for future events, or what we may find in that place were we to revisit. Questions interrogate memory and moment to provide an opportunity for envisioning and prediction. Perceptions, meanings and experiences of place are informed by temporal and spatial connections that are unique to the individual as they meet themselves in the world (Rawlings Smith & Pike, 2024). Active engagement with such reflexive processes can prompt a deeper understanding of how place connection can support creative responses to OL in a range of educational and non-educational settings.

Barriers to Place Connection

Pedagogical choices in OL should be informed by a recognition of individuals' access, experiences and encounters (or not) with nature and the outdoors. The example above implicates inherent privilege and opportunity offered by both the place and people around that experience. I deliberately chose to share a vignette of a place I felt included in and connected to as a child. This draws on a happy memory, despite my experiences of other places which evoke different emotive and interoceptive responses; 'darker' places, where I felt excluded, or which felt unsafe, or experiences I would rather forget. Reflection on your own experiences of place and childhood memories of the outdoors will prompt a range of responses. This is *your* starting point. You may enjoy remembering experiences and find them easy to engage with. You may also meet with emotional resistance or barriers which impact on your engagement. Certain memories could evoke uncomfortable responses, or you may also encounter *disconnection*. You may not be able to recall at all. Interoceptive, sympathetic and empathetic experiences are more difficult to ascertain when we feel 'disconnected' (whether psychologically, physically, spiritually, or emotionally) from the natural world. Places can equally evoke undesired responses related to past, present, or future experiences. Therefore, place-responsive pedagogy must account and pre-emptively plan for expected and unexpected consequences of diverse interactions, connections, or disconnections in different places. It is our intention in this book to provide teachers and education researchers tools to proactively consider how opportunities for OL may be broadened and harnessed for all children and young people to support connection, inclusion and belonging.

Social media and popular imagery 'tell us' how we should feel in nature; a sense of freedom is conveyed by the viral image of the lone mountaineer throwing their arms out wide on a seemingly isolated mountain peak. Likes and shares on Instagram tell you that this is how we should *be* in nature (despite reality behind the lens being perhaps very different IRL [in real life]). Repeated exposure to messaging manipulated by algorithms we ourselves have created commands us to feel awe, wonder and peace as we experience nature's highly filtered beauty – either vicariously through others or directly ourselves. The 'colonisation' of places and 'unprecedented intrusion' of digital technologies on socio-cultural experiences impact on how humans communicate, exchange and process information, learn and navigate their world (O'Connor, 2021). Technological devices mediate our experience of the world around us as social media perpetuates the human need to establish social connections through photographing and sharing experiences as a mode of self-presentation (O'Connor, 2021).

While technology can be an effective tool within OL, experiencing nature 'through a lens' could be argued to prevent true experiential connection, as one of many factors which can influence disconnection from nature. Resultant outcomes of human–nature disconnection through increasing 'technologicalisation of the social', is a result of 'limitless technological expansion and our increasing inability to imagine either ourselves or our world in other than technological terms' (O'Connor, 2021, p. 1). This results in a 'loss of respect, humility, and empathy with nature' via the relative attractions of 'indoor sedentary entertainment' (Zylstra et al., 2014, pp. 119–143). In this scenario, we may spend more time scrolling through heavily edited images of other people's natural encounters on screens than time connecting with nature ourselves. Research has shown that 'greenfluencers' promoting environmentally conscious lifestyles on social media, can encourage pro-environmental behaviours (Boerman et al., 2022). However, the 'influencer effect' of viral images of wild natural spaces not only impacts on the place itself (sometimes to its detriment, as beauty spots and fragile ecosystems become overwhelmed with selfie-seeking individuals), but also raises awareness around how we could reconnect with nature by seeking out such opportunities. This may remove barriers to disconnection as we are motivated to access nature to feel good ourselves. Place-responsive pedagogy in OL can offer ways to balance technological interactions whilst maintaining a human-nature-world-centred perspective which focusses on authentic relationships established through shared experiences. Beyond this, *more-than-human* relationships are realised as the individual interacts within and responds to the world around them (Abram, 1996).

The psychological construct of 'nature connection' emphasises the importance of the human–nature relationship through establishing and maintaining 'pathways to nature connectedness' which include direct sensorial experience, emotional connections, meaning, aesthetic appreciation and compassion (Richardson et al., 2020, p. 387). One well-cited study of nature *disconnection* is Louv's (2005) non-medical diagnosis of 'nature-deficit disorder', which highlighted increasing trends in reduction of time that children spend outside and linked detriments to human health and wellbeing. A broadly termed 'nature' is widely accepted as a therapeutic antidote to 'attentional problems, depression, anxiety, obesity, and impaired social development' linked to an urbanised childhood 'heavily indoctrinated into the web of technology' (Hechter & Fife, 2019, p. 45). Resultant effects include uncomfortable relationships with nature versus 'nature connectedness' (Pritchard et al., 2020) and nature-colonisation. It is important to note that nature-deficit disorder has been criticised for its assumptions of 'a fall-return narrative' separated from the 'psychological, interpersonal, and cultural fracturing [which] promote disconnection in the first place' (Dickinson, 2013, p. 328). Dickinson reframes this issue of *disconnection,* demanding an 'inward expansion' of the human–nature relationship where we 'go inside (psychologically, culturally, and relationally) and ask the difficult questions' surrounding the diverse and idiosyncratic connections between humans and natural places (2013, p. 330).

Practitioners entering the field of OL need to understand that children's feelings of 'disconnect' result in a lack of belonging in a space. This raises barriers to learning and participation. Chapters in this book take up Dickinson's challenge by looking closely at the ways that people and places relate to different connections established through experiential learning, social and environmental interactions. Interrogation of connection/disconnection can guide us to question norms and values (*doxa*) perpetuated by education systems and symbolic power to cement of 'a sense of one's place' (Bourdieu, 1984, p. 141), further elucidating understandings of place-responsive approaches in OL.

Understanding Place on a Socio-cultural Plane

Bourdieu's notions of *habitus, field* and *capital* (Bourdieu, 1977) provide anthropological insights to approach the necessary complication of place. These 'open concepts' can support an ontological approach within OL, answering Akram's (2023) call to 'take Bourdieu into the world' (p. 211). Conceptual frameworks related to Bourdieu's theories have been applied to educational research in different ways. Extending use of Bourdieu's Theory of Practice (1977–1990), the analysis of structure and individual agency is particularly insightful to choices we make around place-based pedagogy. This provides an understanding of the dynamic interplay between individual, experience, culture and context.

The concept of *habitus* supports an understanding of how people engage with different places, given existing 'systems of durable, transposable dispositions' reflecting 'the internalisation of externality and the externalisation of internality' (Bourdieu, 1977, p. 72). In any given place, interactions and relationships will be influenced by 'predispositions' and 'embodied practices' of individuals which are a result of their background, experiences and position in the world (Bourdieu, 1977, p. 72). It is, therefore, important for educators to understand place – or the *field* – as the site of experience we ask individuals to enter to 'experience' or 'encounter' in OL.

However, it is also important to understand that individuals are not subject to a place, nor is a place subject to human action; but by entering any place, we establish a space for *social action* and exchange. Place is given meaning and value that people as *agents* will interpret differently given the set of dispositions they draw on (Bourdieu, 1977). Motives, feelings and relationships are constructed and reconstructed through experiences in different contexts that are intentionally and strategically negotiated although such interactions and interpretations may occur unconsciously (Akram, 2023, p. 190). This provides insights into different sorts of *capital* resulting from the development of habitus and how this is selected, evolved, adapted and built over time in one or more places. For Bourdieu, relational space is determined by the different positions of those entering them: 'such fields are characterised by struggles over capital and authority' (Akram, 2023, p. 191). In OL situations, we need to therefore question dynamics of power and interplay of agency versus space. This questioning can lead to *transformative* practice (Bourdieu & Passeron, 1990; Freire, 1996, 1998).

Questioning our assumptions of what we 'think we know' will happen in a place-based encounter requires us to not only focus on individual agency but also the site of action itself. This entails a deep understanding of *doxa*: the taken-for-granted practice enacted within the field that is guided by our own habitus. Ascribing to OL as an agreed 'good thing' (*orthodoxy*) also invites debate, critique and different interpretations (*heterodoxy*) to question what may be taken for granted by the practitioner due to their experience of how 'the natural and social world appears as self-evident' (*doxa*) (Bourdieu, 1977, p. 164). Reflexive practice is, therefore, an important part of OL as we shift from observation of *what* we notice taking place, to understanding *how* this happened and *why*. This entails recognising temporal and spatial transitions transcending the site of experience, 'while also maintaining a focus on the present as "practice"' (Akram, 2023, p. 203).

What do I know about this place, and where has this knowledge come from?

What do they know about this place and how was their knowledge formed?

How will this place shape, guide and inform interactions? How can I plan for new discoveries to create new connections?

Akram (2023) asks us to recognise that 'habitus must be *brought forth* because it is often taken-for-granted rather than assumed' (p. 203, original emphasis). Her 'six-point heuristic' (Fig. 1.2), a proposed methodology for analysis of narrative interviews, can also be useful to guide reflexive practice in OL:

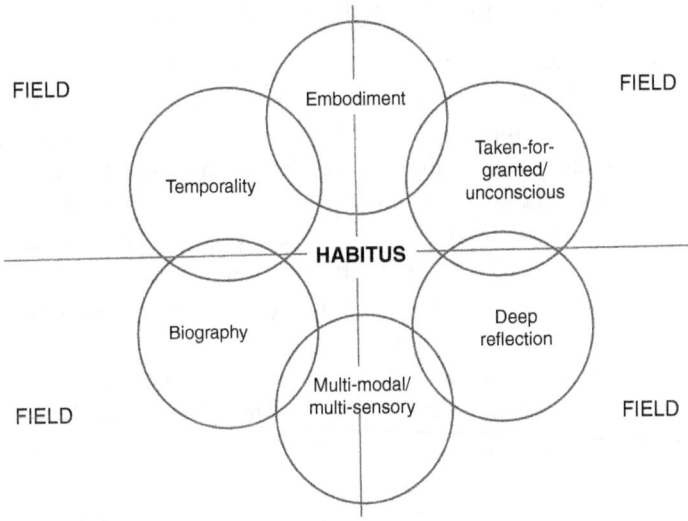

Fig. 1.2. Habitus as Method: Internal Components and Field (Akram, 2023, p. 206).

Applying Akram's model to the vignette of the 'fallen tree' offered earlier in this chapter, experiences in the outdoors can be viewed through the lens of habitus as a multifaceted concept. Place-based encounters are intertwined with *temporality* (moment, memory, duration, frequency) and *embodied* through *multi-modal, multi-sensory* psychological and physiological responses (physical, cognitive, emotional, interoceptive, interceptive). They are informed by what we *take for granted*, as well as *biography* (history, narrative, language, *doxa*, society and culture) and involve *deep reflection* upon all of this to enable reflexivity and agency. Cognitive, social, emotional and physical connections are, from this perspective, established through different spatiotemporal experiences, both shaped and influenced by the individual (habitus) and the place(s) (field). Choices of theory, practice and pedagogy are thus formed. 'Place' may be reimagined as a socio-material, sociocultural construct rooted in multiple and sometimes conflicting dimensions of time and space: in past experiences of other places, in future desires for sustainable environments, in present concerns such as peeling satsumas in a fallen tree.

Place-responsive Pedagogy Within OL

Placing a greater emphasis on a 'pedagogy of place' contributes to students' engagement with educational practice (Wattchow & Brown, 2011) and benefits professional practice in addressing educational disconnection. From the perspective of place as socio-material and socio-cultural webs of activity (enrolled in multiple times/spaces), place-responsive pedagogy can be used as a lens for practice in OL. It offers the capacity to speak to the diversity of outdoor educational practice, ideology and experience without curtailing or limiting it.

Whatever the reader's intention or aims, adopting a place-responsive pedagogical approach offers food for thought around how to plan at a deeper level for education outdoors, through developing an awareness of how learners may relate to different places. Developing awareness of learners' connections benefits education planning in several respects. Perhaps foremost is consideration of the intertwining relationships between people, materials, history and cultures which pre-exist and will continue to be formed within and beyond the physical site of the planned learning activity – informing *capital* and transforming *habitus* in various *fields*. Educators should consider the centrality and inescapability of learners' involvement in cultural place-based activities and their interaction with socio-cultural-material worlds which entangle in the development of subjective attitudes and dispositions to place.

A place-responsive approach to pedagogy, thus, draws heavily on a notion of place-connection as *storying*; this is underpinned by the belief that narratives reside in places and people. Stories of the world, as lived experience, play a significant role in outdoor experiences (Wattchow & Brown, 2011). Applying place-responsive pedagogy, thus, involves careful consideration of potential experiential, sensory and affective products of *being* and *doing* in different places, and how these aspects may be woven into a child's story of place. This becomes a shared story of *place-making*: an intentional act of actively shaping and using a specific physical environment as a key component of the learning process. Unique characteristics and stories of place can be integrated into teaching and learning activities to deepen learners' understanding and connection to their surroundings. Planning, therefore, needs to take a holistic and interdisciplinary view of place.

This is particularly pertinent where wider social and cultural trends meet socio-political experiences in education. OL situated within current concerns for world-centred education and environmental education brings a heightened need for practitioners to consider the wider social and political discourses of sustainability that students are impacted by but might not directly experience. Disconnected dystopic visions of climate catastrophe in widespread media can be connected to learning about renewable energy in STEM lessons exploring wind turbines, for example. Or, perhaps, we may discuss the conundrum of peeling a satsuma that has been transported thousands of miles by air freight whilst sitting in a fallen tree connecting with an environment significantly changed through intensive livestock farming. Through authentically situated encounters, children connect directly to a place, on this planet, to learn how to care for it and nurture its regeneration. In such examples, pedagogy must consider implications of how wider political trends may impact children's ability to connect and the type of connection wherein education is planned.

Personal and ethical associations with place have implications for children's development of identity and representation of self in relation to the world. Belonging and connectedness to the world are established through meanings ascribed to and interpreted by the individual through the lens of the social and cultural fields they inhabit. Therefore, each instance of place-responsive pedagogy may be better understood concerning associations of socio-material, socio-political and socio-cultural influences which have created relationships to place, rather than primarily about curriculum-based aims 'taken outdoors'. This is a flipping of priorities rather than a replacement: seen as a cultural, holistic and continuous process, OL may be explored as a *critical* pedagogy of place (Gruenewald, 2003; Wattchow & Brown, 2011), expanded on more deeply through each chapter in this book.

Recent developments in educational research advocate for 'slow pedagogy', developed from Froebelian principles (Clark, 2021), and 'world centred education' (Biesta, 2021), which foregrounds the development of the individual's subjectivity over (a trend for) foregrounding qualification in education systems (Chapter 2). Addressing issues of inclusion/exclusion, critical place-responsive pedagogy supports educators in recognising the bio-psycho-social-cultural needs of learners situated in different places, at different times. It is through such processes that an inclusive and holistic approach to OL can be developed, placing the individual and the socio-material world they inhabit at the centre of practice (Chapter 3).

Learning is situated in complex and recursive relationships between people and resources; 'the social life of things' whereby things are full of people and people are made through interaction with things and other people (Appadurai, 1988). The social implications of resources – how a child will use a stick, what serendipitous learning results from encounters with mud, how complex concepts can be understood from resources brought to a place in a bucket – extend beyond the physical site of the educational activity to assignations of meaning developed through socio-material and sociocultural interactions in other times and spaces (Chapters 4–6).

Educators may, thus, begin to consider more astutely the specific practices, knowledge and experiences they intend to offer and its benefit to teaching and learning both now and in the future (Chapters 7 and 8).

Conclusion

The practice of *slow, connected and situated pedagogy* as a key approach in OL could 'ensure encounters between children and curricula in order to encourage and equip them for their own life, which is a life that always takes place in the world' (Biesta, 2025) and may answer critiques to the lack of embedded practice around 'world-centred education' – Biesta's recent contribution to 'educational vocabulary' (Biesta, 2025). This situates the teacher as a mediator and facilitator of the student's connection with, and understanding of, the world around them, built through careful sculpting of lived educational experiences. It is as an 'intervention in practice' (Biesta, 2025) that place-responsive pedagogy in OL can develop world-centred education beyond rhetoric. From such developments, actioned in the field, we envision the role of teachers as 'pedagogues': facilitator, observer and interpreter of connective experiences, supporting learners as they explore and connect with nature. This may provide positive outcomes regarding pro-environmental behaviour and well-being as well as children's cognitive, social, physical, moral and emotional development (Martin et al., 2020). A place-responsive pedagogical framing of learning outdoors provides opportunity for more coherent and planned teaching outside the classroom and for OL to become an established part of curriculum provision and children's learning more widely.

CHAPTER 2

Decolonising Outdoor Learning: Developing Connectedness Through Place-responsive Pedagogy Beyond the Early Years in England

Lucy Sors and Louise Whitfield
York St John University, UK

ABSTRACT

This chapter explores connections between child development, culture and place-responsiveness in outdoor learning (OL). Theoretical influences are traced from historical to contemporary educational thinking. Expanding the conversation beyond the Early Years (EY – 0 – 5 years old), this chapter embraces *connectedness* to inform place-responsive pedagogy and places a lens on Indigenous and local knowledge in curricula in Wales and New Zealand. Our broader aim is to adopt a decolonised, global view of place-responsive OL. This entails considering how different knowledge and values can provide children with opportunities to 'meet themselves in relation to the world' (Biesta, 2021). The challenges of negotiating this 'meeting' relate to broader socio-cultural and socio-political and environmental structures which shape outdoor encounters. This chapter expands a socio-cultural analysis to propose that slow, place-responsive pedagogy should be valued beyond the EY in England.

Introduction

This chapter introduces connectedness as a key feature of place-responsive OL, viewed through a socio-cultural lens. We introduce key theory and research to invite the reader to explore different perspectives and consider how curricula can be designed in response to place. Our analysis emphasises decolonisation in OL, acknowledging theories from different cultures that appreciate the inseparable connection between human–nature relations (Adams et al., 2023). The merging of perspectives invites an ongoing, shared discourse of OL as an opportunity for whole-child development. This sits within a broader vision of connected, sustainable educational practices that can be enabled through conversations with, in, and around different places. Active engagement between learners, educators and the environment itself generates rich and meaningful experiences that promote a deeper understanding, critical thinking and stronger connection to the natural, and human, world.

This chapter will guide the reader to explore how OL contributes to world-centred education (Biesta, 2021) *in practice* and how socio-cultural analysis of *doxa* (taken-for-granted, unquestioned beliefs and values) (Bourdieu, 1977 – see Chapter 1) can elucidate factors impacting children not just as learners, but as agents in the formation of their world now and in the future. World-centred perspectives call into question how knowledge valued by education systems prevailing in England and many other countries is learnt, performed and reproduced from birth (Bourdieu & Passeron, 1990). Namely, the narrow focus on pre-determined 'goals' that children must meet at certain ages. This could be construed as symbolic violence (Bourdieu & Passeron, 1990), which contrasts with play-based, child-centred theories of education promoted by alternative pedagogies. Our conversation extends beyond the typical vision of OL as restrained to the Early Years (EY) to prompt the reader to consider how practitioners can facilitate dialogic, connected and responsive pedagogy for all ages. This supports children to consider how they exist within, respond to and encounter the world (subjectness, Biesta, 2021, p.55), and is the critical 'gesture' of world-centred education; an approach that seeks to provide space and time for us to 'think and look; think and look again' (Gourlay, 2023, p.975).

Theories and Perspectives Informing Place-responsive OL

Histories around the development of OL in the UK note the influence of philosophies emerging from industrialised European economies in reaction to deprivation of liberty, green space and freedom in the 19th and 20th centuries (Oglivie, 2013). Such theories addressed the perceived gap between what children 'need' in terms of contact, relationship and connection with nature, and how this was threatened in pursuit of progress. Educational ideas promoted nature's potential to 'heal' this loss, but in doing so, objectified nature as a resource, rather than viewing it as a partner. Other knowledge systems sustained nature–human connections as part of broader education value-systems viewing 'nature as teacher'; wisdom that has been predominantly overlooked in the prioritisation of western educational theory (Adams et al., 2023). The establishment of OL as a designated category could therefore be viewed as a feature of modern western education in response to 'indoorisation' of education (Neill, in Waite, 2017, p. 57). We first examine how place-responsive pedagogy can be informed by theories and practices emerging in the development of western EY education, before considering conflicts around this within current curriculum design in England.

Our journey begins with an introduction to Friedrich Froebel (1782–1852). Froebelian principles emphasise children's autonomy, connections to the world and individually paced development and continue to inform EY educational practice today (Froebel Trust, n.d.). Froebel supported the idea that early childhood should be 'valued for its own worth in the present' (Froebel Trust, n.d.), conflicting with notions that EY education is to prepare for the next stage in learning. A 'here and now' Froebelian outlook advocates practice around authentic, connected, situated experiences through which children discover interrelationships inherent in different places. This saw development of the 'Kindergarten' (Garden of Children) in

1837, to foster children's engagement with nature. Outdoor encounters responding to different places, involving independent discovery and play are a key part of the Froebelian vision of child development, as connections are built through experiential learning (Bruce, 2011). Transcending experiences, children connect within 'their living core' to the universe around them (Froebel, 1826 cited in Froebelian Futures, n.d.). Froebelian practitioners support 'unity and connectedness' by enabling children to learn in a holistic way (Froebel Trust, n.d.). Approaches include developing situated dialogue between the child and world, facilitating understanding of their place within it. This frames child development as a search for meaning: the child 'meets the world' on their own terms, driven by external and internal forces to engage in meaningful exploration.

The notion that children can self-direct their journeys through the world has been critiqued for its limitations, not least of its applicability to all children in all societies. 'Re-imaginings' (Sakr & Kaur, 2024) of Froebelian philosophy seek to question Froebel's original vision of the role of 'guiding' adult who 'naturally hits upon the right thing to do' including providing 'gifts' (physical objects designed to facilitate interactions) (Sakr & Kaur, 2024, p. 924). This paradox conflicts with Froebel's ideals of fully independent, creative 'self-education' through the natural world. It also assumes that adult instinct will effectively guide and provide in alignment with children's internal drive to explore. Yet if adults have not experienced freedom of exploration in their own childhood, praxis may clash with this ideal. However, as the EY sector has evolved, Froebel's influence has too, 'as a sprawling, endless and dynamic web of encounters over time and space' (Sakr & Kaur, 2024,). What has endured within EY practice is a commitment to enabling children's self-expression and pedagogy that is fundamentally driven by a powerful urge to learn through interactions in different places. *Learning* in this sense is not achievement of predetermined goals, but rather a movement of thought through interconnected networks of experience, enabling exploration of temporal and spatial interactions beyond immediate contexts.

Environmental connection, which underpins place-responsive practice in OL, was further developed through Maria

Montessori's (1870–1952) influence. Montessori education emphasises the importance of providing a range of activities in the context of real-world situations. Pedagogy situates practice within planned environments that are designed to support children's independence. Montessori's focus on authentic encounters within a given place is 'based on understanding that children have an innate capacity to learn and educate themselves when placed in an environment that allows independence and the freedom to work at their own pace' (Bradley et al., 2011, p. 71). The development of independent skills is supported through adult–child interactions 'following the natural rhythm of each individual' (Isaacs, 2012, p. 97) and *responding* to this. However, emphasis on individual achievement and independence has been critiqued for negating the importance of collective experience, which could be addressed through sociocultural understandings of place. There are evident links within place-responsive pedagogy and Montessori principles of connectedness: learning is connected within children's authentic experiences as a 'meaningful whole' so that new ideas can be linked to what they already know (Tovey, 2017).

Philosophy evolved from Montessori principles through the 'curiosity', or Reggio Emilia approach, developed by Loris Malaguzzi (1920–1994). This emphasises children as autonomous 'powerful partners' who actively co-construct curricula alongside adults. Adults are conceptualised as 'researchers', who follow children's interests, then provide resources and encouragement (provocations) to explore these further. The child is the starting point for an *emerging* curriculum, designed to respond to their interactions and connections to places, spaces and objects (Bradley et al., 2011). Responses invite ways to stimulate children's curiosity; although these might be adult-driven, children's interactions are not (Strong-Wilson & Ellis, 2007). The flexibility of environment means that place becomes an intrinsic part of the learning experience as children's connections are facilitated through design and provision of *provocations* and '*Pregazzioni*' (projects). These are negotiated and co-constructed between children and 'researching' adults, in different places, over different timescales, with different people. Whilst resource-intensive in its initial stages, many outdoor educators apply Reggio Emilia 'curiosity' approaches to use the environment as 'third teacher' (Strong-Wilson & Ellis, 2007). *Provocations of place* incorporate Montessori approaches of authentic encounters alongside Froebelian 'natural' explorations of places, with attention to 'slow' practices which provide time for children to learn, without pressure of reaching predetermined outcomes.

Western visions of 'The Outdoors' supporting health and wellbeing through space, interaction and exploration, informed educational practice in response to conflicting societal demands. In early 20th-century Britain, women advocating for social justice had significant influence on practice. 'Free flow' access to outdoors, still prioritised in EY settings, derives from the Macmillan sisters' influence (Rachel, 1859–1917; Margaret, 1860–1931). Their open-air nursery was established to support children's health and wellbeing in poverty-stricken inner-city London. Practice related to 'schema' (repeated actions and behaviours that children use to learn) was developed by Susan Isaacs' (1885–1948) use of 'big ideas' in learning environments which contain 'rich treasure chests' of exploration (Woods, 2017, p. 12). Child-centred, play-based and experiential pedagogy continued to evolve in EY settings, developing perspectives on 'learning by doing' from liberal theorists such as John Dewey (1859–1952). Theory and practice derived from trailblazers in EY pedagogy inform philosophies of place, pace and play in OL.

Evolution of fundamental educational theory continues, not least from critiques of theories and ideas presented above. For example, Biesta's (2021) 'world-centred' vision for education challenges 'child-centred' (*ego*logic) theories to expand beyond the individual. This suggests 'active redirecting' of children's attention to the *world* (*eco*logic) so that they can respond to what the world is asking of them. This perspective informs education within a sustainable future and aligns with knowledge underpinning EY principles linked to exploration, enquiry and freedom. Expanding a broader vision around existing theory to address limitations in its cultural applicability, contemporary conversations around 'unity and connectedness' (Froebel, 1826) centre on rediscovering our relationships to the 'more-than-human-world' making use of Indigenous and local knowledge (Abram, 1996; Taylor et al., 2012). Recognising the 'co-existence of a diverse plurality of forms of knowing, being and doing' (Gabi et al., 2023, abstract), questions western notions of 'The Outdoors' and recognises academic dependency on western theories of education which inform OL theory and practice. Recent critique around narrow views of learning suggests alternative socio-cultural approaches around 'different focal planes' (Waite, 2017, p. 10).

We turn to examine relational, cultural, psychological and experiential connections within OL, which have mainly been forgotten in performance-driven educational systems prioritising structured learning indoors (Waite, 2017). Place-responsive OL supports renewed perspectives on fundamental theories and principles which can reignite situating practice *around* the child within different places in a quest for slow, sensitive and responsive pedagogical approaches. As the reader engages with this with chapter, it might be useful to consider *'what we have forgotten'* within current discourses in education. Through such reflexivity, we seek to reprioritise powerful connections within OL, extending key EY principles outlined above to apply to all children of all ages. This re-establishes *place as teacher*, enabling children to meet the world, themselves and others.

Play and Learning in the Outdoors: Conflicts Within the English Education System

Despite wide recognition of its benefits, OL continues to be overshadowed by current neo-liberal foci on attainment, 'learnification' (Biesta & Priestley, 2013) and performance, which reproduce a 'banking model' of education (Freire, 1996). Measurement and reporting of 'learning' from EY and throughout education, continues to emphasise children acquiring *knowledge* over a *process* of 'meeting' the world and themselves (Biesta, 2021). The 'prevalence of performativity' (Biesta, 2021, p. 99) conflicts with children's natural propensity to explore, experience and 'be' in a place, as they develop world-self-others connections. Performativity subsequently leads to a growing loss of ontological security for teachers; both a loss of sense of meaning in what they do and what is important within their role (Ball, 2013). The extent to which theories and ideas presented above are realised in practice, and continued beyond the EY, is constrained by demands of current curriculum design. Post-EY practice continues to be reliant on structural-constructivist theory around the 'more knowledgeable other'. Whilst EY approaches place value on adult–child relationships, they extend beyond this to nurture children's independent, creative and symbolic discovery and connection to the wider and natural world (May et al., 2006). This aligns with socio-cultural perspectives which seek to emphasise the power and importance of child-led play (May et al., 2006).

A Froebelian vision of play 'helps children to relate their inner worlds of feelings, ideas and lived experiences taking them to new levels of thinking, feeling, imagining and creating' (Froebel Trust, n.d.). A wide range of literature supports holistic benefits of outdoor play (Ardelean et al., 2021; Marchant et al., 2019). However, play declines from EY to upper years of primary education in England, and outdoor play becomes mainly confined to short breaks away from academic learning, threatening freedom and connections to nature (Marchant et al., 2019). 'Piecemeal offerings' of play have declined significantly over a quarter of a century (Baines & Blatchford, 2023, p. 15), with the 'brutal' loss of time and space for play impacting on pupils' experiences and enjoyment of school as well as their wellbeing and mental health (Grant et al., 2024). Limited access to outdoor spaces impacts children's realities in their daily lives (Grant et al., 2024). In a longitudinal study of play in English schools, Baines and Blatchford (2023) cite that the main reasons for decline relate to time pressures and beliefs around behaviour management. This is at odds with research suggesting that play *is* a form of learning; providing important contexts for development of positive behaviour, health and school engagement (Baines and Blatchford, 2023). Play needs to happen beyond asphalt-bound, heavily supervised and time-restricted breaktimes to discover potential and boundless possibilities offered by open-ended learning through interactions outdoors.

Outdoor play beyond EY can be informed by theories introduced above, which communicate the importance of freedom, natural environments and resources to encourage complex, collaborative, creative and varied interactions with the world (Ardelean et al., 2021). In England, the concept of 'free-flow' in the EY curriculum envisages children developing ownership of experience to freely imagine and explore their interests, thoughts and feelings through 'flow' as they become intensely focussed and absorbed in play (Bruce, 2011). However, this prompts critique of how play-based learning appears in practice. The Early Years Foundation Stage Framework (EYFSF) contradictorily states that 'children learn through play, by *adults modelling*, by observing each other and through *adult-guided learning*' (DfE, 2024a, 2024b, p. 7 – *our emphasis*). Conflicting curriculum guidance driven by prescribed outcomes and statutory assessments restricts and controls time, space and ownership of play (Bradley et al., 2011, p. 79), at odds with genuine, self-led learning. Instead, responsive, connected approaches to learning provides open exploration and unplanned conversations in different spaces (Hughes et al., 2018), supporting new perspectives on how play can develop children's *ecologic* understanding through situated interactions. Such experiences are important to socio-cultural learning that should be valued throughout childhood. Playful, authentic and connected pedagogical design can similarly inform educational curriculums beyond the EY.

Theories of individually paced development and concepts of stage/age conflict in the English educational system. Measurements of child development 'milestones' are closely followed by concepts of 'readiness' for Key Stage 1 by age 5 (DfE, 2024a, 2024b). The ensuing educational system (ages 5–18) increasingly prioritises a *logic of progress* towards marketplace goals (Gilead, 2012). This values predetermined *stages* of learning over non-linear, messier individual development and self-exploration. There is a focus on 'preparedness' of 'essential skills and knowledge' in specific areas of learning determined by the National Curriculum (DfE, 2014). The shift from play-based pedagogy to formal teaching and learning abruptly steers learners away from free-flow experiences towards external drivers preparing them for 'expected' achievement and outcomes.

The EYFSF is the first of what can be seen as a 'data delivery chain' through the education system (Roberts-Holmes & Bradbury, 2015, p. 313). This reflects notions of an 'accelerated childhood' (Clark, 2023). A centralised, prescriptive approach may be viewed as 'stunting the potential of children by formulating their learning in advance' (Soler & Miller, 2003, p. 66). There are implications of symbolic power and subjectivity here, as explored by Bourdieu and Passeron (1990) in the cultural role of 'pedagogic action'. This theory unpicks the imposition of policy directives where children are subject to pre-determined learning objectives and notions of what education should be: reproducing 'cultural codes' already dominant in the system. Against the neoliberal backdrop of performativity, practitioners are also subject to such 'symbolic violence' (Bourdieu & Passeron, 1990) as their responsibilities of nurturing child development through care and guidance are replaced with understandings of education around academic progress. Expanding EY principles to inform educational as a *process* considers authentic, world-centred approaches. Learning at any age cannot be compartmentalised into 'strands' or 'subjects', nor can learning be confined to a single setting with a pre-determined assessment-driven agenda. Instead, each experience, in every place, is richly, intrinsically *connected* to another. This supports a renewed vision of connected, gentle pedagogies which slow down approaches to education.

Slow Pedagogy and Fostering Connection

The 'hurried' nature of the current English education system, as echoed in many other western education contexts, may mean that time is not given to allow levels of absorption which foster connections to people and places. Time must be afforded to attend to the 'urgency of slow' (Clark, 2021). Building on Payne and Wattchow's concept of 'slow pedagogy' as an important feature of post-traditional outdoor education (2008), Alison Clark explores what this looks, sounds and feels like in EY settings:

- valuing the present moment
- being attentive to children's pace, rhythm and interests
- enabling children to revisit their ideas and creations, places and stories

- creating opportunities for children to go deeper in their learning
- supporting time for observation, listening, reflection and documentation
- encouraging unhurried everyday routines with time for wonder and care

(Clark, Froebel Trust, n.d.).

Interviewing experts in the field, Clark (2023) examines different imaginings of slow pedagogy. 'Slow' is juxtaposed against 'fast pedagogy': driven by the need to get somewhere for a specific time. Connected, compassionate pedagogy is at the heart of slow approaches, where adults work in partnerships with children, grasping opportunities to go 'off-track' to explore different possibilities (Clark, 2023). Around situated encounters in the present, a 'rhythm' of connections is established between individuals, materials and place: an 'idea of "being *with*"' (Kind in Clark, 2023). Applying slow pedagogy to OL establishes *being with* nature as opposed to being *in* nature; a reciprocal relationship between child and the natural world and inseparable from temporality (Payne & Wattchow, 2008). This views *places as partners* which connect to the world *here and now*. Subjective experiences evolve from place-responsive encounters that inform a unique journey between the child and the world, taken in different directions over different amounts of time.

It is questionable whether children have opportunities to develop opportunities to 'meet the world and meet themselves in relation to the world' within the hurried nature of our education system (Biesta, 2021, p. 8). A slow approach is *responsive* to the world, situated in different places that allows children to develop personal knowledge (Dubiel, 2023) and connections that go beyond knowledge prioritised within curricula directed by standards and 'learning goals' (EYFSF, DfE, 2024a, 2024b). Curiosity-driven approaches enable children to explore the world in their own time, at their own pace to their own level. Such immersion enables whole-child development through connected experiences in different places. *Time for slow* in EY and beyond can meet needs, interests and rhythms of the 'unique child' (DfE, 2024a, 2024b). There is potential for *slow* to inform ideas in the EYFSF such as the 'Characteristics of Effective Learning' (CoEL) (DfE, 2024a, 2024b), and into the primary and secondary curriculums, allowing time for learners to 'approach opportunities with curiosity, energy and enthusiasm' (DfE, 2024a, 2024b). Challenge, exploration and passion to learn about the world through 'curiosity' could reframe learning as a connected and transformative process. This places a lens on *how* we learn through interactions with the world and how *the world* impacts these interactions. Connections between learners, places and relationships require educators to adopt a patient approach, foster slow enquiry and enact deliberate and mindful choices (Clark, 2021, 2023).

Indigenous and Local Connections for Place-responsive OL

From a critical decolonised perspective, it is important to recognise that western theories popularise philosophy already inherent in other knowledge systems. A westernised concept of 'outdoor learning' might be framed differently, but it connects to ideas of place-based encounters which are an innate part of growing up in different societies across the world. A sense of connection with the natural world beyond the human perspective is upheld as a cornerstone of educational practice found in many cultures (Adams et al., 2023). With the emergence of transdisciplinary co-exchange, local and Indigenous knowledge systems can inform how intergenerational knowledge is reproduced within global communities (UNESCO, 2002–present). Such knowledge places cultural value on holism, nature-connection, paced and place-based learning and should not be co-opted or misappropriated. Challenging UNESCO's view of Indigenous knowledge transmission being 'complementary' to mainstream education, we instead make the case for how this should be jointly considered with other perspectives to play an informing role in establishing world-centred educational approaches and advance educational practice (Waite, 2017, p. 65). A 'glocalised' interplay challenges curriculum approaches to learn from 'place- and local-based pedagogies' (Waite, 2017, p. 65), whilst meeting the specific needs/deficits of the English educational system. Cultural transfer informs the transformative potential of educators' use of shared cultural capital to improve pedagogy (Mills, 2008 drawing on Bourdieu & Passeron, 1990). Interactions with the world are fostered through interconnected, embodied, biographical, reflective, sensory, spiritual and cognitive experiences.

A decolonised approach to outdoor and place-responsive learning can enable a deeper understanding of values permeating our own educational contexts. This supports a critical challenge to dominant pedagogies. We explore underpinning values within two bilingual National Curricula: Early Childhood Curriculum of New Zealand 0–4 Years (*Te Whāriki*) (Ministry of Education New Zealand (MENZ), 2017) and the Curriculum for Wales 3–16 years (CfW) (Welsh Government, 2022). Recent challenges to colonisation within these countries have resulted in recovery of hitherto marginalised wisdom from local and Indigenous knowledge, language and values. Hence, we show how '*what we have forgotten*' can be actively addressed by revisiting meanings of place within policy. Engagement with different socio-cultural perspectives represented in these curricula support an understanding of how culture and field influences *doxa:* the implicit beliefs, values and assumptions which underpin fundamental principles of educational discourse (Bourdieu, 1977). This focus responds to Biesta's articulation of what 'education' is, and what it should be about: 'Education also has an important role to play in providing the new generation with orientation into the traditions, cultures, and practices of past and present. This is the important and difficult work of *socialisation*' (Biesta, 2021, p.7–8, *original emphasis*). Biesta notes the 'difficult' nature of this work for educators, not least that we may ourselves be playing into complex 'socialisation agendas', but also 'because it raises all the complex questions of how such traditions, cultures and practices can be (re)-presented in the curriculum, how we can make meaningful selections, knowing that it is not possible to (re)present everything to everyone' (Biesta, 2021, p.8).

With this in mind, our analysis centres on two key terms embedded in language, thought and culture that are implicit in *doxa* within the two curricula: *Te Whāriki* (New Zealand) and *Cynefin* (Wales). These warrant further attention due to their socio-linguistically symbolic nature. Critiques and histories of *Te Whāriki* have been explored elsewhere, noting tension around its initial theoretical beginnings conflicted with notions of developmental and cultural appropriateness (Ritchie, 2018; Soler & Miller, 2003). *Cynefin* has attracted recent attention during the rewriting of the Welsh Curriculum, with a range of perspectives 'exploring ideas on belonging, connectedness and community' published in the British Educational Research Association Blog series (May 2024). In our analysis, we examine how these core concepts transcend educational settings to embrace language, culture and place. Summarised below, *Te Whāriki* and *Cynefin* provide a social semiotic lens into 'ways of knowing and states of being' (Adams et al., 2023, p. 23) that are alternative to dominant discourses in education. We invite the reader to consider how these values can inform a renewed perspective on OL and educational curriculum design.

Te Whāriki

Te Whāriki's literal translation is 'woven flax mat', 'which can be woven by different groups to create their own "distinctive patterns" derived from different cultural perspectives, philosophical emphases, community priorities and organisational differences' (Ritchie, 2018, p. 130). The metaphor supports a social-cultural and ecological model of early childhood education. Spirituality and ancestry within Te Whāriki support a sense of belonging emphasising connection within societal values. The mat supports 'weavers' of practice to design the curriculum around the child to empower them with cultural knowledge, skills and attributes they need to be active contributors to society. A deeper analysis views the 'mat' as enabling all stakeholders; teachers, educators, families, communities and children, to 'stand' together on it: the woven strands provide strength to support them. In the published curriculum booklet for Te Whāriki, the metaphor is expanded by colour, design and symbolism to communicate the foundations and process of learning and potential in children's ongoing learning journeys (MENZ, 2017).

Cynefin

Cynefin is described in the CfW as 'the historic, cultural and social place which has shaped and continues to change the community which inhabits it' (Welsh Government, 2022). Cynefin could be conceptualised as a 'being of place' (Adams, 2023), where humans connect and participate within the world through a grounded and reciprocal relationship. Cynefin 'speaks of having a relationship with the land and a strong sense of place' and acknowledges that a 'sense of identity is enmeshed with a sense of place and is of existential significance' (Adams et al., 2023, p. 13). Cynefin underpins the CfW as a driving concept to support curriculum outcomes in relation to heritage, community, language and diversity (Welsh Government, 2022).

Cynefin and Te Whāriki are fundamental principles based around community, culture, relationships and place which echo a vision for a world-centred view for education. Through a closer analysis of how these principles inform curriculum design, we explore how they support children to 'meet the world' and 'meet themselves in relation to the world' in space and time to understand 'what the world is asking' from us (Biesta, 2021). Themes for analysis expanded below support a broader, decolonised vision of world-centred education can inform place-responsive pedagogy in OL.

Eco-systems of Community and Culture

Bronfenbrenner's ecological systems theory (1979), alongside Bourdieu's concept of *doxa* (1977), can support an understanding of how *cynefin* and Te Whāriki link to children's holistic development. Their influence permeates interactions and connections between the layers of curricula interpretations. *Doxa* moves between systems from the *macro* (country, culture and language), *exo* (governments, curricula documents and guidance), *meso* (community, communications, connections) and *micro* (educational setting, home, neighbourhood, family), to which the individual is both a recipient and a donor of interactions. Collaboration between educational settings, families and communities features in both curricula, connecting partnerships in education. Autonomy of educational providers is emphasised within both frameworks, where bespoke design of curriculum responds to local priorities.

In Wales, a community-responsive approach is embedded within the concept of *cynefin* which is both shaped by and shapes its unique community (Welsh Government, 2022). The design of the CfW intends that schools and communities work together to co-construct their own curriculum in response to the needs of the locality, yet a significant paradigm shift is required for this to be fully realised in practice (Tyrie & Brinn, 2024). Te Whāriki similarly acknowledges that educational settings are rooted in culture, communities, and includes wider ancestral concepts of families. It emphasises the importance of strengthening children's sense of belonging as intrinsic to happiness and well-being. Te Whāriki explicitly embraces an ecological systems model, which views development as influenced by interconnected relationships: 'Children's learning is located within the nested contexts and relationships of family, community, and wider local, national and global influences' (MENZ, 2017, p. 60). The 'interwoven mat' metaphorically represents connectedness through symbolic portrayal of society's 'weavers' supporting and empowering children to develop cultural and educational knowledge. Situating learning within community and responding through an informed *sense of place* is a key feature of both curricula. This highlights the importance of responsiveness to context, by building connections to the local environment, people and culture within OL.

Belonging to and Being in the World

Belonging features strongly in the concepts of *cynefin* and Te Whāriki, extending beyond community to encompass the intangible relationships that are established between the child,

Earth and beyond, through developing a knowledge of their own place in the world (MENZ, 2017, p. 90). Connections and interrelatedness emerging in both curricula aligns with theories of 'unity and connectedness' presented earlier. Developing a sense of connection and belonging to others and the environment, children develop through 'engaging in meaningful interactions with people, places and things – a process that continues throughout their lifetimes' (MENZ, 2017, p. 12). This challenges *ego*logic practice to explore existential connections and probe questions of our 'subject-ness' in *eco*logic, world-based encounters (Biesta, 2021). 'Being' in the world requires educators to support exploration of how the world 'asks' individuals to be present by 'finding the place where they can be found' (Biesta, 2021). Contemporary educational research is beginning to engage with concepts which explore notions of learning within the 'more than human world' (Abram, 1996). This centres practice 'beyond the autonomous individual child' (Taylor et al., 2012, p. 81), to become aware of reciprocal interdependencies and interrelatedness:

> *They experience not being in a place but feeling part of a place. In doing so, they develop their awareness of ways of knowing and states of being that are not usually prioritised in schooling in industrialised societies. Feeling part of the more-than-human world helps to cultivate a sense of relationship that not only benefits future human and planetary wellbeing but also fosters enhanced existential understandings (Adams et al., 2023, p. 23).*

Cynefin and *Te Whāriki* embody 'ways of knowing' as children develop their understanding of the natural world having existential significance to their lives, their place in the world and their value within it. In the CfW, *cynefin* supports connections to a broader vision of the world; beyond place, nation, culture and language and 'the place where we feel we belong' (Welsh Government, 2022). Enquiry, curiosity and problem-solving are supported throughout. An emphasis on world-connection is communicated through different 'types of value' that will support 'sustainable development and the challenges facing humanity' in 'changing local, national and global contexts' (Welsh Government, 2022). Ownership and autonomy of powerful knowledge and its application places individuals as agents, who can enact change in an ever-developing world. Approaches in *Te Whāriki* have a similar emphasis on the power of the individual, providing children with regular opportunities to connect with their environmental responsibilities and to observe nature without harming it (MENZ, 2017). Depth of respect for place and a sense of belonging to not only this time, this place, but also beyond space and time is emphasised through Indigenous knowledge roots and links to the spiritual realm (MENZ, 2017). Emphasis on connection in both curricula establishes a notion of 'boundary-less exploration', through which a sense of deep belonging is established (Adams et al., 2023).

Connectedness and Responsive Curriculum Designs

Te Whāriki and *cynefin* recognise that 'children learn through responsive and reciprocal relationships with people, places and things in their world' (MENZ, 2017, p. 60). Place-responsiveness in curriculum design, therefore, plays a key part in how children develop world-connections.

Both curricula connect to the importance of authentic learning environments that facilitate interactive and relevant learning opportunities. Connections are established through the learning *process* and development of skills, which recognises and respects the place of the child in the world now and in the future. 'Integral skills' feature in the CfW, which enable pupils to see 'beyond knowledge as being a list of unconnected facts' (Welsh Government, 2022). This vision emphasises the importance of ensuring that learners are equipped with skills and *space* to 'generate creative ideas and to critically evaluate alternatives' (Welsh Government, 2022) in response to local, national and global priorities. Within *Te Whāriki*, the bicultural nature of New Zealand is celebrated through mapping of 'strands and threads' which reflect and respond to changing needs, interests and priorities (Soler & Miller, 2003). Diversity of practice is informed by local 'character' of culture and place (Sobel, 2013, p. 31). Responsive curriculum designs will have limitations, both on engagement with partners and value-driven decision-making which influences priorities in the design of learning (Tyrie & Brinn, 2024). However, designing curricula which is responsive and flexible to individual, community and global needs can support children to develop an awareness of their place in the world and their impact within it (Sobel, 2013).

At its heart, *cynefin* intangibly connects curriculum to local knowledge of land, people and place (Adams, 2023). Similarly, *Te Whāriki* grounds Māori understandings of the intimate connection between nature and humans. Yet connectedness is not conceptualised as a static force; it evolves as the world moves through continual cultural and global change. This is the transformative potential of place-responsive pedagogy: through encounters in different places, adults and children co-interpret and negotiate the world leading to generation of new ideas. Social connections are, therefore, as important as natural connections, as children develop resilience, skills and knowledge to be able to live within, protect and contribute to the world.

Conclusion: Towards Decolonised Place-responsive Pedagogy in OL

This chapter has proposed how different perspectives can inform *connected* place-responsive pedagogy supporting children's experiences in their 'meetings' in the world. Education is viewed as inherently intertwined with relationships, culture and environment. Values of holistic child development permeate all perspectives presented here. Pedagogical choices must support their individual needs and physical, emotional and social wellbeing. These values can be maintained whilst implementing a global, ecologic vision, supporting children to understand and answer to the world as part of their individual developmental journey, extending far beyond the EY.

Too often, in too many places, the powers within curricula rush children through the world, focussing on outcomes over experience. But unhurried, connected and place-responsive pedagogy can address conflicting priorities between world-connection and performance agendas. A slow approach invites children to create their own stories of place in peaceful, unhurried encounters which support them to meet themselves in the world. (Biesta, 2021). Connections to, within and beyond places, space and time are, thus, realised. This challenges neo-liberalist policies and accelerated notions of childhood (Clark, 2021) to support a more compassionate approach to pedagogy, with connectedness valued as central to developing the 'whole child' and supporting them to find their place.

Integrating a 'decolonised perspective that acknowledges Indigenous wisdom and reveres beings in nature as subjects and our relations' (Adams et al., 2023, p. 13), requires renewed focus on the role of *place* as an active 'teacher' to support individual, local and community priorities through observation, interaction and respect for the natural world (Sobel, 2013). Deep and meaningful connections to outdoor places can be developed by encouraging children to explore, play and question. Outdoor pedagogy is therefore first and foremost about creating or finding places for 'playful encounters' (Woods, 2017). Play, viewed as symbolic interactions of cultural learning, can support exploration of different feelings about, and experiences of, the same place, whilst 'slow' methods develop children's – and our own – values and connections. Through dialogue and interaction, the teacher becomes co-learner, researcher and facilitator as they intentionally engage and participate alongside children to enable co-constructed learning journeys in different places. Reciprocal exchanges, relationships and encounters inform tailored responses to place. Knowing *how* to respond requires 'listening' and acknowledging interactions on a human and more-than-human plane suggested by places, people and objects (Taylor et al., 2012).

Connectedness is a subjective experience that is unique to an individual's relationship with the world. OL practitioners, therefore, need to gain a holistic understanding of systems which interact with individuals and transcend environments. Critical, responsive pedagogy has the potential to address inherent socio-cultural barriers and contribute to curriculum visions that value children's experiences *here and now*, as explored in the next chapter. The challenge put forward here is to consider how place-responsive pedagogy can facilitate a decolonised approach informed by culture and critical theory, to build connections based on deep appreciation and respect of the world.

CHAPTER 3

Inclusive and Holistic Practice in Place-responsive Outdoor Learning

Lucy Sors
York St John University, UK

ABSTRACT

This chapter aims to promote inclusion in outdoor learning (OL) through practice that empowers agency, access and participation. Embracing learning as a cultural process, inclusion in OL recognises and supports diversity through pedagogical design that responds to people and places. Meaningful processes of co-construction provide insight into how OL can embrace individual interests and identities, inform expectations and support anticipatory planning within critical, holistic and adaptive practice. The chapter places particular focus on including children and young people with Special Educational Needs (SEN) and/or disabilities through pedagogy that celebrates and understands difference. I introduce 'critical adaptive pedagogy' and other practical tools to suggest how barriers can be anticipated, identified and addressed to plan inclusive OL environments and experiences. This involves a continuous cycle of co-construction, anticipation, planning, response and critical thinking. The chapter exemplifies a holistic and inclusive approach that can be applied to any context and every individual, to ensure that *all* learners can access and participate in meaningful, challenging OL opportunities.

Introduction

> *Every young person should experience the world beyond the classroom as an essential part of learning and personal development, whatever their age, ability or circumstances (Learning Outside the Classroom (LOTC) Manifesto, DfES, 2006, p. 1).*

The conviction of the philosophy communicated in the LOTC Manifesto poses a pertinent challenge to educators; how can we include *every* learner in OL? To address this, I propose that inclusion in OL can be informed by *place-* and *person-*responsive approaches. Diverse responses to the outdoors draw attention to factors influencing connections to and within the (s)p(l)ace of learning (spatial-temporal experiences of place) and suggest *active noticing* of individuals' different interactions (Mason, 2021). An emphasis on individual agency recognises that experiences of place are encountered differently due to subjective corporal, cognitive and emotional connections (Payne & Wattchow, 2009). Following Grunewald, this entails knowing how 'our cultural experience is "placed" in the "geography" of our everyday lives, and in the "ecology" of the diverse relationships that take place within and between places' (Gruenewald, 2008, p. 137). Challenging former deficit models of difference, inclusive practice responds to diverse ecological relationships that transcend different places. This starts with authentic, meaningful processes of co-construction designed to provide insight into different individual 'geographies', to build on their strengths and recognise and address barriers inhibiting access, participation and enjoyment.

One aim of this chapter is to address issues around inclusion and diversity that are under-researched in OL literature (Kelly et al., 2022). Therefore we begin with a broad reflection around developing inclusive cultures in OL, considering how this is shaped by policy, research and theory in the field of inclusion. The focus then moves to adaptive practice for diverse learners who encounter barriers due to difference and/or disability. In England, the associated term 'Special Educational Needs and Disabilities' (SEND) appears within policy and guidance referred to in this chapter (UK Parliament 2014; Department for Education (DfE), 2015). This is named differently elsewhere in the UK (e.g. Additional Support Needs [Scotland] or Additional Learning Needs [Wales]). Despite semantic differences, a shared understanding communicates the necessity to enact *additional and different* support to address barriers and enable Children and Young People (CYP) to reach their full potential. There is wide recognition that effective inclusive systems value the unique contributions that students of all backgrounds bring to education and that benefits for all learners can be realised by enabling diverse groups to grow, develop and learn together in different settings (CAST, 2024; DfE, 2014; UNICEF, 2017). I apply this principle to explore how this can be achieved in OL.

Tools presented in this chapter support a mindful approach and critical reflection on *why*, *what* and *how* inclusion occurs in different places. These holistic methods support different layers of practice from universal support to highly personalised individual support. Barriers can be addressed through a process called *adaptive critical pedagogy* (Sors & Bloom, 2024) which advances discourse on 'adaptive teaching'. This starts by recognising the importance of positive responses to difference through attitudes, values and expectations. At the heart of inclusion in OL lies continual and critical reflection that evolves our practice. This involves 'learning from attempts to overcome barriers to access and participation and make changes everybody can benefit from', and valuing differences as 'resources to support learning, rather than seeing them as problems to be overcome.' (Booth and Ainscow, 2011). Alongside theory, policy and research, this chapter is informed by my personal and professional experiences as a teacher and Special Educational Needs and Disabilities Coordinator (SENDCo) collaborating with CYP and their families, and as a parent negotiating my own children's barriers to participation in an ever-changing world. Ideas presented over the next pages are designed to support the reader's consideration of inclusive and holistic approaches that could be applied within their own practice to support *all* CYP to participate and be successful in OL.

From Inclusion to Meaningful Participation

Inclusion is a broad term, with a range of interpretations and implications. Despite enduring acceptance of the need to advocate for 'inclusive education to create an inclusive society' (UNESCO, 1994, n.p.), there is still debate and confusion as to how to address the 'challenge of inclusion' (Ainscow, 2024, p. 1). Broadly, inclusion emphasises the importance of access, equality and promotion of diversity regardless of difference and is underpinned by concepts of social justice and Human Rights. Research, policy and practice in the field of Equality, Diversity and Inclusion (EDI) is designed to protect against discrimination and promotes reform in culture, education, policy and practice to empower oppressed groups (UNESCO, 2020). Continually evolving critical theory around race, gender and disability asks us to recognise and challenge socially constructed understandings. These derive from the *doxa* of dominant discourse (see previous chapters) and result in implicit bias and beliefs that underpin long-standing exclusionary practices.

In OL, representations of place, history and people are of particular concern. Legacies of colonialism, slavery and racial violence, gender, socioeconomic and ableist bias have shaped cultural understandings of the outdoors and 'determined who should and can have access to natural spaces' (Finney, 2014, abstract). This compels us, within our practice, to narrate unequal power structures and discern 'hidden' histories of place which have been overshadowed by hegemonic systems. Bodies of research which tackle critical pedagogies of place seek to 'decolonise and reinhabit the storied landscape' (Johnson, 2012, abstract) through mindful, direct engagement and confrontation of injurious, exploitative and exclusive past and present histories. 'Proactive teaching to transgress repressive myths and praxis' is needed to challenge embedded assumptions around history and culture (Warren & Breunig, 2019, p. 6). Contesting areas of exclusion and oppression in OL demand deep, targeted conversations (see Finney, 2014; Gray & Mitten, 2018; Johnson, 2012; Waren & Breuning, 2019). The 'challenge of inclusion' regarding neurodiversity and disability also needs to be addressed more thoroughly in OL literature. An 'unending process of inclusion', can be harnessed to challenge inequality, address barriers, meet needs, fulfil rights and provide a range of opportunities for success (Ainscow, 2024; Booth & Ainscow, 2002). This turns our attention to how policy, research and practice can support inclusive processes within OL.

In England, policies such as the Equality Act (2010), Children and Families Act (2014) and Special Educational Needs Code of Practice (SEND CoP, DfE, 2015) have the potential to be powerful, informative tools to support co-creation, advocate for EDI and protect against discrimination. However, 'on the ground' action is affected by local pressures and interpretations (Ainscow, 2024). This results in conflicting experiences of CYP with SEND and frustrations felt by them and their families about the need to 'battle' for appropriate support (DfE, 2023, p. 3). Based on the latest SEND reviews in England, co-creation and participation are threatened by lack of trust and an inconsistent, inefficient and disordered SEND system (DfE, 2022; House of Lords, 2022). The very legislation designed to promote advocacy for inclusion has suffered significant 'failure of implementation' (House of Lords, 2022, p. 79), and many CYP with SEND support have been reported as 'having a very poor experience of the education system' (OFSTED, 2021).

Action is needed to address barriers to opportunity and increase participation by responding to the diversity of CYP in any given context (Booth & Ainscow, 2011). The *SEND and Alternative Provision (AP) Improvement Plan* (DfE, 2023) proposes reforms which have yet to be fully implemented at the time of writing. There is an 'urgent need' to reform the system, and, as initiatives such as specialist units in mainstream schools and the expansion of AP are established (UK Government, March 2025), an opportunity for renewed approaches to enhance high quality provision for pupils with SEND should consider the importance of OL in its design. As an alternative to typical educational approaches, OL can seek to increase participation of all pupils in diverse experiences. OL can play its part to rebuild confidence and trust by implementing equal, consistent support and sustaining effective provision that is accessible to all. It is in outdoor situations that as a SENDCo and teacher

I have frequently experienced the growth in trust from CYP and the development of relationships built on mutual respect. Interacting together outside offers different opportunities for engagement, building connections and experiences of success. Through sharing experiences that celebrate CYP's diverse responses within low-threat, natural environments, we can start to rebuild aspects of trust that may have been undermined by an educational system reliant on meeting unachievable targets, or where opportunities for genuine participation and partnerships have been missed.

Policy and guidance in England emphasise maintaining *high expectations* which 'inspire, motivate and challenge (…) pupils of all backgrounds, abilities and dispositions' (DfE, 2011–2021). Teachers' *values* and *attitudes* around inclusion are also recognised as 'a key determinant in the school experience of pupils with SEND' (Standard 8: Professional Behaviours, ITTECF, DfE, 2024b, p. 26). There is little guidance as to exactly *what* values and attitudes will inform *what* expectations in any given environment; there is an assumption teachers will have strong theoretical knowledge of what this means. Policies do, however, highlight that values related to inclusion should *identify* and *remove* barriers affecting CYP on an individual level: a 'one size fits all' approach will not meet specific needs (Ainscow, 2024). Guidance also broadly recognises the importance of 'high quality' or 'quality first' teaching (DfE, 2011–2021, 2014, 2024b; EEF, 2021) which engages all learners through a range of pedagogical methods that are designed to build on their strengths, support their needs and remove barriers to participation. Expectation should, therefore, be centred around how to increase learner agency by design learning environments that are 'accessible, inclusive, and challenging for every learner' (see Universal Design for Learning [UDL] Guidelines, CAST, 2024).

Application of the previous UDL framework to inclusion in OL is explored by Kelly et al. (2022). Pertinent to discussions already developed in this book, Guideline 7 of the UDL Framework communicates the importance of *welcoming interests and identities*. Educators are encouraged to 'nurture playfulness' that encourages opportunities for 'exploration, experimentation and discovery', where space is created for 'learners to find joy through connections to their identities, sense of self, and communities'. (CAST, 2024, consideration 7.3). Designs for OL can embrace these ideas and respond with flexibility to learners as they interact in different ways through playful encounters in different places. Learners' experiences and interactions should lie at the heart of *high expectations* and inform cycles of robust evaluation and planning. Such cycles first consider the impact of high-quality OL practice implemented at a *universal* level for all CYP as well as what *additional and different* support might be needed for individuals.

The culture change brought about by the implementation of the 2014 Children and Families Act requires a focus on children's outcomes and higher levels of participation in decision-making for CYP with SEND. This supports CYP's agency by purposefully enabling their capacity to actively participate in making choices about their learning and education. OL practice should therefore embrace values of co-construction and work collaboratively with CYP to design opportunities for learning and explore expectations and aspirations. Mutually formulated expectations within OL can be designed around what learners know about themselves, what they would like to achieve and what barriers to learning and participation they may encounter in different places. Choice and autonomy are at the heart of reflective, responsive and *reasonable* practice, enacted according to the legal principle of 'best endeavours', which places a proactive duty on educators to make all reasonable efforts to meet individual needs (DfE, 2015; UK Parliament, 2014).

Establishing inclusive cultures in OL demands genuine, consistent and trusted processes for meaningful participation. We therefore enable opportunities to listen to CYP's wishes and learn about their needs, through engaging in dialogue, play and direct consultation. Authentically shared decision-making results from open dialogue that respects and empowers the voice of CYP in inclusive design for OL. Aspiring to reach the top of Roger Hart's (1992) 'ladder of participation', CYP can be enabled to take the highest level of control over their experiences in OL and have a genuine influence over decisions that affect them. This could be as simple as CYP choosing places to encounter, or as progressive as handing over curriculum design to pupils. *Co-construction* challenges deficit views of SEND and begins by presuming CYP's competence, strengths and capacity. This informs a robust system of support that responds to individual needs and addresses barriers (Darling-Hammond, 2020, p. 98). OL can thus facilitate place-based encounters where differences are celebrated and valued, where CYP engage actively as agents and where connections are established and sustained through relationships and partnerships.

Taking an 'Inclusive Turn' in Place-responsive Pedagogy

Ainscow's (2007) 'inclusive turn' encourages problem-solving within a collaborative culture, moving beyond inclusion as 'enabling access' to consider specific influences on *connection*, *belonging* and *engagement*. This involves deeper understanding of structural, social, political, environmental and economic factors and their influence and informs how we can strengthen connections to foster belonging and community in OL through multiple means of engagement for *all* pupils. In doing so, we 'acknowledge the remarkable variability in what attracts and engages learners' interests and what constitutes an environment that affirms the dignity of every learner' (UDL, Guideline 7, CAST, 2024). The focus is holistic, informing continuous, agent-led processes of inclusive practice *on and around* groups, individuals and places.

Interactionist models such as a bio-ecological system view established and evolved by Bronfenbrenner (1994) consider how community, environment, place and people interact and shape each other over time. Individuals are both 'influenced and influential within the nested social system (…) of dynamic interconnections' (Elliot & Davis, 2020, p. 1121). We can, thus, examine sociocultural influences contributing to CYP's experiences, knowledge and feelings about different places whilst sustaining the value of whole-child development as a continual and dynamic process (Woods, 2017, p. 108). Elliot and Davis (2020) critique the human-centric nature of Bronfenbrenner's model and highlight its limitations in the unsustainable era of the Anthropocene; they propose a revised view to include *non-human* interrelationships. This directs our focus to *place* and *human–nature* interconnections and mutual influences between individual/environment over time. By making *place* the site of inclusion, a holistic, multifactored perspective enlightens complex 'layers' of influence around CYP which 'invite, permit or inhibit engagement' in different environments (Bronfenbrenner, 1994, p. 39).

A revised 'more-than-human' ecological approach can support inclusive practice in place-responsive pedagogy, where factorial *interactions* and *outcomes* can be analysed on spatial and temporal levels. These entail complex reciprocal exchanges which form interrelationships between process, person, time and context (PPTC) or 'proximal processes' (Bronfenbrenner, 1995). Proximal processes within an environment (both immediate and more distant) play an active role in CYP's interactions at any given moment (Bronfenbrenner, 1995). Therefore, place-*responsive* pedagogy must build flexibility around dynamic relationships between PPTC to consider how best to enable inclusion. Within the field of experience, flexible and responsive practice 'in the moment' entails critical 'active noticing' (Mason, 2021) of interacting PPTC factors that negatively impact on access, engagement and enjoyment of OL. This transcends space and time as we develop a deeper understanding of barriers around, within and outside different places. We plan to address these to improve CYP's learning, relationships, well-being, agency, experiences and, ultimately, life chances.

Sobel calls for educators to 'unshackle' from the restrictions of mandated curricula to enact 'place-based education' which establishes connections to support CYP to develop values, skills and knowledge relevant to their lives both now and in the future (Sobel, 2013, p. 12). Educational practice is informed by the local 'character' of curriculum, culture and place but also the need to respond to the uniqueness of individuals within any given past, present or future context. 'Changing participation' (Sobel, 2013, p. 31) is, thus, a key consideration for inclusion in OL. Place-responsive pedagogy starts with pupils' active engagement with local priorities before expanding to care, respect and action in the wider world. This prioritises CYP as 'co-constructors, active creative social agents' (Cosaro, in Elliott & Davis, 2020, p. 1121) whose interactions have impact.

Individuals are not 'subject' to systems, place or circumstances, but play a symbolically active part within them (Bourdieu & Passeron, 1990). If we question 'symbolic power' (invisible, taken-for-granted hierarchical power structures influencing perceptions and values), meaningful participation can be enabled, and *transformation* is possible (Bourdieu & Passeron, 1990; Freire, 1998).

Negotiating power structures involves challenging understandings, assumptions, implicit bias and stereotypes which we have come to accept as truth. Thus, inclusion and social justice in OL involve critical reflection on one's own worldview through an 'epistemological lens' (Warren & Breunig, 2019, p. 5). Questioning our privilege and positions as educators is important; such reflection prompted me to recall an early career experience teaching in an area of high socioeconomic deprivation. I had planned a speaking and listening activity to introduce sequential sentence starters (first, then, next, finally, etc.) using photographs of me walking in a local woodland. It soon became apparent that this context was unfamiliar to many pupils as they struggled to narrate the pictures. I had assumed that given the school was situated near woodland, children would have previously walked there and would relate to the picture-story scaffold. Recognising my assumption, I looked to OL as a key pedagogical approach to provide tangible encounters to support learning based on children's *own* experiences. Their recounts developed into rich, authentic and personal narratives, supporting the development of vocabulary and deep, meaningful and memorable learning. Over time, pupils took ownership of OL encounters to direct and initiate interactions as their confidence developed in new and different places. *Transformation* occurred to support pupils' meaningful participation as part of usual educational practice.

Inclusive practice in OL acknowledges that CYP have diverse starting points which shape their encounters. Interpretations and interactions are as varied and unique as the individuals and the places they experience. Perceptions of OL must, therefore, be carefully unlocked to add value to individual experiences and responses. Active engagement with a reimagined bio-ecological systems view (Elliot & Davis, 2020), can identify CYP's existing relationships (or lack of) to different places through collaborative consultation. Appropriate place-situated learning opportunities can then be identified, developing anticipatory and sustainable OL planning that builds on strengths and addresses potential barriers. Practice, thus, evolves and adapts to changing concerns on ecological systemic levels. We first examine the *chronosystem* in terms of how strengths/barriers emerge, develop and change over time in response to different environments, and how environments change in response to interactions with CYP (e.g. adjustments, adaptations, impact of 'being' in a space). *Macrosystems* clarify socio-cultural norms, beliefs and values of the community, religion and language of which the CYP is a participant. This may shed light on different perspectives of OL and related activities (e.g. connections to nature or messy/muddy play). The *exosystem* elucidates interactions and influences between society/individual in terms of how ideas around inclusion are perceived, assumed, constructed and communicated (e.g. positive or negative messages about needs, disability, identity; intersectionality; what CYP 'can' or 'can't do in different places). The *mesosystem* informs interactions or experiences within local surroundings and proximity to this (e.g. access to, or exclusion from, outdoor contexts). The *microsystem* reveals people, peer networks, strengths, needs and interests of the CYP that shape an essential part of the 'jigsaw' to inform inclusive practice in OL. Here, connections (or disconnection) between the individual and the non-human world can be explored as part of their 'local biosystem' which recognises CYP's 'capacities to drive agentic change that may ripple outward' (Elliott & Davis, 2020, p. 1138).

A broad vision for inclusion in OL is based on shared, achievable expectations relevant to individuals, their interests and their connections and interactions with the world. This is informed by the individual's socio-cultural journey alongside their neurobiological, social, physical, cognitive and emotional development and relationships with different places. Transformative practice in OL embraces an 'inclusive turn' by identifying barriers to learning and participation as a dialogic, dynamic process. Next, we consider how pedagogical methodology can support this process.

Introducing Adaptive Critical Pedagogy in OL

Critical pedagogy, pioneered by Paulo Freire (1921–1997), challenges existing power structures and inequality to empower learners to become active participants and creators of knowledge. *Adaptive* critical pedagogy asks educators to actively challenge exclusionary practices by responding to emerging interactions, maintaining focus on empowerment and agency. This starts with presumption of competence and commits consistently to co-construction, as knowledge is developed through joint problem-solving. As a continuous, responsive process, educators consistently adapt their practice according to emerging strengths, needs and interactions. This will vary according to place, process, person, time and context. Enactment of practice will determine whether CYP will be included (or excluded), experience success (or failure) and develop connection (or disconnection) within OL. Adaptive critical pedagogy is illustrated in Fig. 3.1.

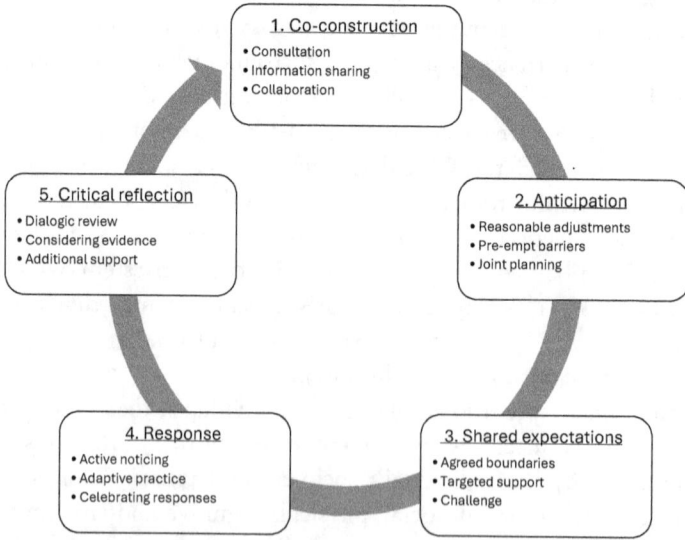

Fig. 3.1. Adaptive Critical Pedagogy.

To apply this in a practical way, consider the questions below which could be used in your own collaboration and consultation with CYP to provide insight into their strengths, interests experiences and needs. Depending on context, this may entail meeting to share information in traditional formats, but, more effectively, information gathering can be gained through ongoing dialogue with individuals or groups to enable insight into areas of difficulty and/or difference which impacts on their participation, enjoyment and learning. This provides a positive starting point for co-construction (1) and questions will become more specific as relationships develop:

- *Who are they? (socio-cultural background/identity/intersecting dimensions)*
- *How do they communicate? (e.g. language/visuals/sign/technology)*
- *What do they like? (interests/preferences/strengths)*
- *What don't they like? (aversions/triggers)*
- *What do CYP and their parent/carers say they want or need?*
- *What aspirations and expectations do they have now/long-term?*
- *What has worked in the past? What is working now?*

Information sharing provides solid foundations for anticipatory planning, building on strengths, supporting needs and providing challenge with a specific focus on OL. Joint planning informs pre-emption of barriers (2):

- *What experiences, environments and resources will respond to diverse learners' strengths, interests and needs?*
- *What reasonable adjustments are needed?*
- *Are there any barriers to accessing the situation, encounter or resources?*
- *How familiar are they with OL, this place or this activity?*
- *What are existing relationships like?*
- *How can I improve accessibility and anticipate further barriers?*

Continuing processes of participation establish shared expectations (3). Expectations and boundaries related to safety and belonging (examined in greater detail later in this chapter), as well as specific approaches and targeted support to address anticipated barriers are reflected on, discussed and agreed. This includes ensuring that planned activities will provide adequate challenge, in line with *high expectations* which inspire and motivate CYP to engage and experience success (DfE, 2021).

- *How can they feel safe – how have risks been assessed and responded to?*
- *What expectations are there around boundaries? (environmental/personal)*
- *What will this encounter look like, sound like, feel like?*
- *What do they want to achieve?*
- *How confident do they feel?*
- *What additional and different support is needed?*
- *How can we make use of tools, resources, support and the environment to set challenges beyond initial expectations?*

Responsive practice (4) builds on expectations and is explicitly linked to these. This entails *active noticing* (Mason, 2021) of learners' emerging responses as we engage by being fully present with them in and with a place (Mason, 2021; Wattchow & Brown, 2011). Tailored adjustments provide options for future actions; practice is clarified and informed through ongoing research and consultation. Adaptation becomes second nature as practitioners develop their inclusive practice repertoire to make decisions based on knowledge about CYP and *their* responses; 'what matters is *knowing* – to act in the moment' (Mason, 2021, p. 232). This includes adjustments such as changing language, approach, resources, PPTC and level of support and challenge to improve individual experience. Diverse responses are celebrated through engaging in individual and collective reflection. This becomes something we do *anyway*, not 'in addition to' (Sors & Bloom, 2024).

The final stage of the cycle is an important element of *critical* adaptive practice (5) a *shared* process of reflection considering 'evidence'. This is enabled through analytic, formative assessment, which is already embedded in our practice, and a dialogic review of experience, connections and encounters that have taken place. A key feature of adaptive pedagogy in the present is a view for the future. Thereafter, further support or adjustments are fed back into the cycle with emphasis on skills for life-long learning to enable access and support aspirations. A sustainable vision for adaptive critical pedagogy prioritises individual empowerment, with CYP valued as active, creative participants in its continuous process.

Holistic Assessment in OL

A holistic assessment tool introduced in this section supports structured decision-making to implement adaptive critical pedagogy in OL. This multi-faceted approach is designed to support conversations and planning to enable a better understanding of the unique circumstances, strengths and needs of each CYP Holistic tools are used elsewhere to support assessment. For example, the triangulated framework in Working Together to Safeguard Children (WTSC) (DfE, 2023, p. 57) encourages practitioners to work collaboratively with families to gather information about safeguarding. Although critiqued for its limited use in social work due to lack of training and low take-up (DfE, 2017), the tool's multifactorial design centres around the child to identify strengths, gaps and needs in safety, welfare and well-being. Deriving its structure from the WTSC tool, the framework presented in Fig. 3.2 supports collaborative problem-solving in OL and is designed to focus considerations around individuals and places, rather than create unwieldy processes of formal assessment which may inhibit a 'full picture' vision of effective inclusive practice. This is not hierarchical, but holistic, and suggests how place-responsive pedagogy can be problematised and adapted to build on strengths and remove barriers for all CYP.

Working in partnership with CYP, carers, professionals and communities, consultation around elements of the triangle in Fig. 3.2 can identify diverse and complex factors in different places to address barriers to participation and learning. It

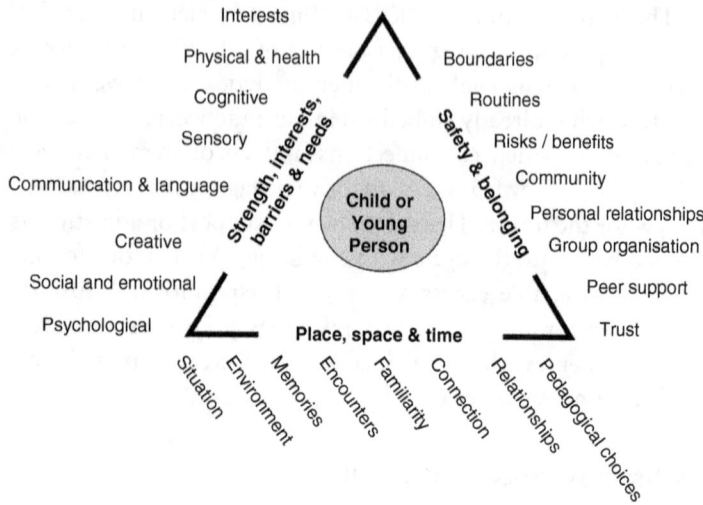

Fig. 3.2. Holistic Assessment in Outdoor Learning.

focusses on three key areas: *place, space and time; strengths, interests, barriers and needs*; and *safety and belonging*.

Inclusive Approaches to Place, Space and Time

The base of the 'triangle' in Fig. 3.2 lists multiple factors to be considered in assessing what may shape responses to OL. Place-based encounters are shaped by lived experiences, informed by interactional and relational activity and environmental factors transcending space, place and time (see introduction, 'Pause for Connection', and Chapter One). Payne and Wattchow (2009) invite us to engage in 'phenomenological deconstruction' to consider how 'embodied sensory-perceptual' factors are unique to individual perceptions of place (p.15). Place connection takes place on a 'corporal level' involving experiences making 'full use of all the senses' (Wattchow & Brown, 2011, p. 182). This requires us to develop critical awareness of interacting factors such as: the situation and its environment (space); memories and experiences shaped by encounters past and present, repetition, or transferability, affecting familiarity (time); and the mutual relationships and connections built between the individual and environment (place). New places, or entering the unknown, can create additional anxieties for CYP. Therefore, experiences and encounters should be planned with sensitivity and informed from an empathetic perspective that recognises the power of memory and impact of present experiences of place. Connection to place is, therefore, a complex web of physical, temporal and relational factors, influencing our choices over where we might situate learning, activities we introduce and the pedagogies we adopt.

If, given phenomenological deconstruction, the environment is filtered through the senses, then attention to an individual's sensory processing is key to understanding how to foster place-connection and reduce anxiety. Attention to sensory demands in any given place can pre-empt barriers and inform supportive practice to overcome them. Activities should, therefore, be designed to support physical and sensory integration, with attention to individual sensory preferences. These should respond to the diverse offerings of a place, making use of multiple ways to engage learners with encounters in the environment that spark curiosity, connection and discovery. OL activities can, therefore, encourage different ways to activate and support visual, auditory, tactile, oral, olfactory, vestibular and proprioceptive sensory systems. A return to holistic approaches and guided participation in activities which place value on elemental play (Woods, 2017), can support CYP of all ages to engage in natural exploration and build connections with place.

Pedagogies that value experiential learning can support building relationships between world-self-others. Concerning use of time, 'slow pedagogies' can support interactions around 'meaning making' that is constructed through slow encounters (Clark, 2021; Payne & Wattchow, 2009 – see Chapter Two). Adopting slower approaches can support CYP to take time over learning, be present in the moment and dwell in a place to develop sensory-perceptual connection. However, being slow may be at odds with ecological systems and proximal processes that have played their part in the developmental journey of the individual. Being slow when life and internal pressures act quickly can be a challenge. Slow pedagogy cannot, therefore, be taken-for-granted to work immediately for every individual. CYP who encounter barriers to executive function, social communication and mental health may respond better to directed time, with clear markers serving as safer boundaries. Time needs to be sensitive to the place and carefully organised and communicated with the individual. Some CYP may respond positively to unmeasured time guided freely by the encounter. Others require structured, rigid routines to support the predictability of the environment. Consulting with CYP to decide how to approach temporality in OL is always time well spent.

Identifying Strengths, Interests, Barriers and Needs

The broad range of strengths, interests, barriers and needs outlined in Fig. 3.2 prompts a significant move away from traditional, medical models of disability or notions of SEND as being situated *within* individuals. A 'bio-psycho-social model' developed by Engel (1977) and reflected in the International Classification of Functioning, Disability and Health (ICF) (World Health Organisation, 2001), recognises that disability is a complex interaction between biological, psychological and social factors. Shakespeare (2022) argues that the 'challenge of responding to disability' requires a holistic multifactorial approach to understand environmental *barriers* alongside different functioning within bodies and minds. The elements presented in Fig. 3.2 prompt a deeper consideration of factors which may impact on individuals in a positive, negative or disabling way. These remind us of the diversity and variability of CYP and how particular attention may need to be paid to some areas over others. An individually informed analysis can 'build on strengths and respond to meet needs that may present in the future' (Shakespeare, 2022); this underpins a balanced approach to OL planning which understands the multifactorial barriers encountered in different places.

Recent emphasis on *neurodiversity-affirming practice* advocates a 'strengths-based approach' tailored to support individual needs which assumes competence, values different communication styles and promotes autonomy (Dundon, 2023; Kapp, 2019). Finding out about the 'assets', interests and strengths of neurodivergent learners can overturn deficit-oriented rhetoric.

In OL, we recognise the individual's unique responses to the outdoors and celebrate the diversity of those responses: *What interests, knowledge and understanding do they have? How do they respond to this place? How can we build on their strengths, talents and expertise? How can they share their understanding with others?* This places the views and experiences of CYP at the centre of practice to look beyond the 'challenge of inclusion' (Ainscow, 2024, p. 1; Kapp, 2019) towards a celebration of diversity:

> *People should exalt in the aspects of their condition which empower them .... that difference is such a valuable tool, an enormous asset (...) It's not something that you're 'badged with'; it's not about what you can't do, it's got to be about what you can do.*
> (Packham, 2018)

Autistic naturalist, Chris Packham (2018) explains that the way his brain processes nature in intense sensory detail means that he sees 'every branch, every trunk; I'm seeing the connections between them'. However, Packham adds that such intensity of sensory information can also be 'utterly overwhelming'. By sharing his passion for nature and disseminating his knowledge and expertise, Packham has inspired others to follow his discovery of the natural world. Positive practice around neurodivergent responses requires a shift towards active noticing, listening and understanding strengths/barriers as well as recognising conflicts between them.

Transformation of *doxa* means recognising that differences are not always 'difficulties', 'disorders' or 'disabilities' – rather differences can be enabling when approached through neurodiversity-affirming practice. This is based on understanding neurodiversity 'as a multifaceted construct encompassing biological, psychological, and social dimensions' which 'challenges the traditional deficit-oriented discourse' (Xia et al., 2024, p. 1). A strengths-based understanding of difference must be at the forefront of OL pedagogy that respects neurodivergent identity and supports positive self-concept to emerge through place-based encounters. Relationships based on mutual trust can facilitate freedom of expression and encourage CYP's own interpretations. Pupils' responses should be built on with respectful, identity-affirming practice to secure a sense of belonging and include difference, rather than trying to change it. This requires a process of *reframing* through responsive practice which emphasises positives and celebrates diversity.

Support, compassion and acceptance profoundly impact the wellbeing of neurodivergent individuals (Di Renzo et al., 2020). To support CYP to develop a positive self-concept, positive framing of difference should be enacted at every opportunity, recognising that others' responses will have impact. Empowerment of difference requires space and access to *be* different; this happens when we enable full participation and experimentation in different contexts. Unique responses to places result in diverse experiential connections that can be framed in creative, authentic and inclusive ways. For example, self-stimulatory behaviour (stimming) could be (negatively) framed as a 'symptom' of an 'unmet need' or (positively) framed as a strategy that helps the individual 'manage' sensory input, anxiety or stress. Framed differently, stimming could be celebrated as accessing strategies to support connections in other ways; engaging in repetitive, pleasurable sensory inputs in response to place is an interaction both within the self and between the self and environment. Individuals' expressive reactions such as silence or noise could be viewed positively (they are quiet – they are calmly listening to birds singing/they are loud – they must feel happy) or negatively (they are quiet – they are disinterested/they are loud – this is disruptive). Or *reframed* by the practitioner as a unique response to place independently expressed by the individual. This 'shift' is a 'respectful, affirming approach that recognises fluctuating capacity in neurodivergent students, and prioritises safety, wellbeing, self-esteem and a positive relationship with learning' (Hammond, 2024). The skill of the practitioner is to respond and adapt to emerging interactions. Allowing time for this is important; impatience to 'move learning on' can often negate CYP's exploration of deep, focused interests they discover in the environment.

Removing the ceiling (quite literally) from classroom-based learning, OL research reveals insights into inclusive practice for neurodivergent and disabled learners which may otherwise be constrained by indoor environmental pressures (Beames et al., 2017; Guardino et al., 2019). The inherent nature of taking learning into an outdoor space can support participation of different CYP and is an effective pedagogy to promote inclusion by reducing multiple barriers (Kelly et al., 2022). But this should not be taken for granted. Anticipatory planning in OL involves developing a 'toolkit' which incorporates a range of specific strategies to adapt practice around *differences* and meet *barriers* in a manner that is informed by research, experience and partnerships. Such ongoing study becomes more focussed as relationships develop over time. This takes place by engaging in participatory approaches and active dialogue to recognise multiple voices and diverse positions. Difficulties are individual; barriers may relate, co-occur or not necessarily be experienced. Therefore, 'what works' for one pupil will not necessarily provide the same support for another.

Current guidance of the SEND Code of Practice (DfE, 2015) outline 'four broad areas of needs' to be planned for: cognition and learning (CL), sensory and physical (SP), speech, language and communication (SLC) and social, emotional and mental health (SEMH). However, it stresses the importance of recognising that for the majority of CYP with SEND, 'needs cut across all these areas and (...) may change over time' and warns of the risk of reductionism due to categorisation. 'Mapping' using shared tools such as strengths/needs profiles can be a starting point to plan for the range of barriers which may be experienced by an individual, in one or multiple areas. This looks beyond medical model labelling and pigeon-holing by diagnosis and instead reconceptualises 'barriers' as dynamic and evolving. Understanding what barriers might look like, sound like and feel like comes from co-constructive conversations with CYP, families and professionals; yet a barrier experienced in one place, at one time may not necessarily be experienced in another. The questions underpinning inclusive practice in OL starts with *what can I do to include all pupils?*

(Universal provision), and moves to *how can I address specific barriers experienced by that individual within this particular place at this particular time?* (Additional and different support).

Inclusive OL 'toolkits' expand as adaptive practice evolves in response to how individuals process, access, respond and interact in different environments and situations. Barriers need to be considered contextually: *what might barriers look like in different learning contexts?* For example, a child who experiences sensory processing barriers in a classroom, which may be related to hypersensitivity to fluorescent lights, buzzing projectors, proximity of people and the restriction of sitting at a hard table on a hard chair, may experience different sensory demands in an outdoor environment; these may or may not result in barriers to participation and engagement. In natural spaces that are difficult to access for wheelchair users, or CYP with mobility issues, we need to ask questions first about the spaces chosen for encounters, and how to make adjustments or alternative choices around the individual, their preferences and the barriers they may encounter in that context. Consideration of *'Diversability'* demands us to examine sensory, tactile and alternative ways to interact with places, which can be planned in accordance with physical, auditory, visual and sensory differences and barriers. And so on. Context and factorial interactions between the individual and place dictate how we approach inclusive practice.

To some extent, the discovery of barriers will require anticipating what may happen in a different context based on what we already know about that individual and their strengths and needs. Such 'detective work' (Trussler & Robinson, 2015) applies a 'social-relational' approach to unpick barriers around encounters and proximal processes (PPCT). The best information we can gather to inform anticipatory practice is from CYP themselves: not what we 'think' we know, but about what *we know* about what *they know*. Place-responsive pedagogy is, thus, *person*-responsive. To inform this, a process of 'empathy mapping' (Gray, 2017) can be adapted for a specific OL context: *active noticing* in each situation considers individuals' observable behaviours (e.g. what they say/do) alongside what 'lies beneath' (e.g. what they see, hear, think and feel). Observable behaviours can, thus, be understood through empathetic approaches that could reveal (unmet) needs or (dis-) connection to environment. CYP need to feel confident so that they can communicate their thoughts, feelings, actions and needs, but this must be taken beyond compassion and into action. Barriers to OL are pre-empted based on 'what we know' and assimilated into planning for *critical adaptive practice*.

Safety and Belonging

The last side to the triangle in Fig. 3.2 highlights the need for OL to support safety and belonging. Belonging is realised by 'the subjective feeling of deep connection with social groups, physical places, and individual and collective experiences' and relates to feelings of value, worth and well-being (Allen et al., 2021, p. 87). Constructions of 'belonging' are, therefore, unique and subject to interactions transcending places and changing over time (Sobel, 2013). Practice needs to strengthen existing positive connections and develop safe, trusting, positive and respectful relationships between individuals, other people and places. Consideration also needs to be given to interacting factors impacting CYP's freedom and engagement, with attention to their ecological system. Connections with the *more-than-human* aspect of place also impact on this. The environment itself communicates implicit messages interpreted by CYP through planned and unplanned interactions: 'you are safe here, you are welcome here, you belong here'. To support belonging, needs need to be met on a physiological, safety and social-emotional level. Examples of questions to inform your reflective practice around this are mapped in Table 3.1:

Table 3.1. Questions to Support Reflection and Dialogue around Safety and Belonging.

Needs	Universal Provision	Additional and Different Support
Physiological Needs	• Have they had enough to eat and drink? Is there food, water and shelter available at the site? • Are they dressed appropriately? Is clothing available in case of changes of weather, etc.? (e.g. getting wet/muddy) • Is there somewhere to cool down, warm up, shelter from wind or the elements, etc.? • Is the site accessible to all CYP? • Does the place offer space for rest, calm and relaxation as well as for play, learning and exploration? • Are medical kits and medicines easily accessible?	• How do CYP communicate/understand hunger/thirst, etc.? Do CYP know where and how they can access food/drink/shelter? • What weather/temperature preferences do they have? Are these accounted for in planning? Is support needed to change clothes? • Are adjustments in place to enable access to the site (e.g. transport) and to all spaces on site? • Do CYP have physical supports/auxiliary aids/medicines on site? • Are individual health needs considered and planned for? (e.g. allergies, physical conditions, mental health conditions?)
Safety and Security	• How does this experience relate to others? • Is OL part of a routine? Has this been followed? • Have all CYP participated in the co-construction of risk/benefit assessment, OL planning and design? • Is a risk assessment (RA) in place? Have you communicated this to everyone involved with the activities? • Do CYP understand boundaries, risks and expectations?	• How can CYP be supported to make links between their experiences to reduce anxiety around unfamiliarity? • Has anything that is out of line with expected routines or any changes been explained and pre-empted as far as possible? • How can you accommodate CYP who find change difficult? • What alternative and different methods of communication will support CYP to understand routine, boundaries, risks, expectations and activities, etc. before, during and after OL?

Table 3.1. (*Continued*).

Needs	Universal Provision	Additional and Different Support
	• How are CYP included to conduct dynamic RA throughout the experience? How are risks communicated and evaluated as they emerge over time? • Are behaviour management approaches designed to meet individual needs? • What contingency plans are in place to support all CYP?	• Does any equipment need to be adapted/alternatives used? • Does the RA account for CYP's needs, e.g. considerations for different behaviour/responses/ additional risks? • Are emergency operational procedures in place to respond to individual needs/ difficulties?
Belonging and Social, Psychological & Emotional Safety	• Have CYP been consulted? Are approaches to OL collaborative, transparent and responsive? • How can everyone's differences be celebrated and valued? • Do CYP feel they can express themselves openly and without judgement? How is this encouraged whilst maintaining boundaries and shared expectations? • Are groups organised to support social integration? Who do they want to be with and what do they want to do? • How do CYP feel about the place/activity/group? • Are relationships based on mutual trust and respect? How are these established and encouraged? • Do CYP know what to do if they get lost or experience something uncomfortable?	• What is special about them? What are their strengths and special areas of interest? How can you build on these? • How can CYP be encouraged to share their expertise and interests in their communication style? • How will you encourage and support different and diverse interactions and responses? • Are CYP with familiar people? Do they have an identified safe person they can go to? Do they want to be on their own? • Are additional check-ins organised to give insight into CYP's feelings? How are feelings shared and communicated? • Is there a safe space established to support sensory over-stimulation or heightened anxiety? (E.g. somewhere dark, quiet, with calming materials – following sensory preferences).

The main idea communicated is how questions can be considered through an inquiry-based approach to establish a *safety net* for all CYP taking part in OL. *Universal* considerations for inclusive OL are presented in the first column, and the second column suggests ideas around *additional and different* support. Pre-emptive strategies support belonging and safety and embed inclusive practice as 'what we do anyway' within OL. Planning may include different adjustments; such as: extra equipment (e.g. auxiliary aids for mobility, communication, sensory support etc.); personnel support (e.g. support staff, additional adults, personal- or health- care support assistants etc.) and methods of communication (e.g. visual, written, verbal, signed communication, use of technology, language etc.). Anticipatory planning relates to physiological needs such as accounting for changes in temperature, weather, hunger, thirst, health, etc., as well as transparent and collaborative approaches to ensure safety and security on a physical, social, emotional, psychological and emotional level.

Co-construction can inform and reduce risks to physiological, physical and emotional safety. However, despite our best endeavours, there will be undoubtedly occasions where the unexpected occurs. We therefore need to prepare to respond in the moment, maintaining a focus on inclusive approaches that support safety and belonging. Risk management, and preparing for the unexpected, becomes a 'fluid, dynamic and relational process' (Garden, 2022, p. 1282) that responds to individuals' interactions within a particular place. With knowledge developed through collaborative conversations, practitioners can organise environments to reduce exposure to threat or harm and address vulnerability, whilst encouraging active engagement with places through challenges where CYP can explore a balanced approach to risk.

Inclusive Approaches to Risk Assessment

Risk-aversion continues to be a barrier to OL; this contrasts starkly with the risk of loss of childhood and risks to well-being associated with 'indoorism' and detachment from the outdoors (Garden, 2022). Risk/benefits risk assessment (RA) analysis recognises the need for risk and challenge alongside potential threats to safety associated with the environment, activities and individual barriers. A 'strengths/needs' perspective can inform this new approach and embed *place-responsive* RA rather than blanket approaches to risk or RA that focuses on barriers and limitations. Horseman (2019) offers an accessible outline to approach RA in the context of Forest School education, which can be applied to other OL contexts. This recognises the need to move away from 'box ticking' to enable risky play as a 'tool for growth' as well as maintaining dynamic ongoing RA specific to context (Horseman, 2019, pp. 162–163). The principles inherent in risk/benefits and dynamic, responsive RA are centred around spatial, temporal and individual considerations. CYP involvement in RA is central to meaningful participation and informs critical adaptive practice around risk.

Co-construction in RA enables CYP to make judgements based on information they gain from others and environment, supporting them to develop ownership of different spaces (Garden, 2022). Co-constructed boundaries should be revisited, reiterated and evaluated frequently with a focus on perceptions and experiences of risk, benefits and success (Garden, 2022). A shared language of *expectation* can develop a realistic understanding of what *will* happen, what *could* happen and what is *expected* in an outdoor context. Pre-emption is key and needs to be shared and communicated with all learners to prepare them to be safe on a psychological and physiological level. CYP with SEND will require adapted strategies in RA that will enable their safety and support their full participation. For some, this might include visual supports to aid social imagination and 'story' the place before an experience. Visual RA uses images from the OL site and show potential hazards, boundaries or areas to be aware of, that can prompt a deeper conversation and understanding of what to expect. Use of photographs, virtual field trips and virtual reality can help prepare CYP for OL and provide ways for them to reach places that are otherwise inaccessible (McDougall et al., 2022). Once in a place, many CYP will respond more positively to calmly repeated, simple positively framed instructions rather than 'controlling and negative language to reprise and instruct' (Horseman, 2019,

p. 162). Communication, thus, plays a central part in fostering belonging and safety.

Approaches to inclusive RA place well-being at the centre of practice and connect to collaborative problem-solving within a world-centred, sustainable vision for education. This requires a flexible approach to support success into adulthood by developing autonomy:

> *(Children) are more likely to experiment and get positive feedback from testing their ideas. This is what governs the development of self-confidence and the ability to solve problems, and as this develops, it allows that flexibility to be internalised by the child, giving them greater capacities to manage themselves in the future and be more flexible, adapting to changing circumstances. This process shows that risk should, and will always be, a dynamic process (Horseman, 2009, p. 165).*

Transparency, flexibility and adaptability support CYP to take 'healthy risks' to secure physical and mental safety and instil ownership over their encounters now and in the future. Pre-emptive planning underpins safety and recognises the benefits of decisions over place, activity and pedagogy that will support the needs of individuals in the immediate moment and longer term. Dynamic, timely responses to people and place build on strengths, interests and engagement and support needs, safety and belonging as experiences evolve.

Conclusion

Inclusion in OL is collaborative, responsive and holistic. The structures, processes, interactions and influences outside and within places inform understanding of barriers and how to address them. Primacy of place is considered alongside the primacy of the individual and their interests, identity, strengths, needs, safety and belonging within different places at different times. Anticipatory planning, flexibility and adaptability develop deeper understandings of individuals' experiences and perspectives. Application of the tools presented in this chapter will enable practitioners to engage in constant cycles of reflection and review (Fig. 3.1) and consider elements concerning OL which may impact on access, engagement and experience of OL (Fig. 3.2), to anticipate and address barriers (Table 3.1). This incorporates a creative and critical process whereby practitioners notice and take account of their evolving professional skills and maintain their research-informed foundations. We look outside, and inwards, challenging and critiquing practice and unpicking decisions to consider why we have done what we did and what impact this has had on the individual.

Adapting practice requires practitioners to 'shape-shift' both in their role and approach to deploy sophisticated, effective, active methods in response to the emerging needs of CYP we work with. This 'discipline of noticing as a method of sensitising oneself to notice possibilities for action' (Mason, 2021, p. 231) is engrained by a critical awareness of situations, interactions and responses as they develop within a given place. Space, time, research and reflection underpin authentic inclusive practice in OL. This is not reactive, but *responsive* practice, informed by a professional habitus which evolves over time.

PART 2

Place-responsive Pedagogy in Action

CHAPTER 4

Building Connection to Place: Time and Space in Place-responsive Pedagogy

Ruth Unsworth
University of Glasgow, UK

ABSTRACT

This chapter explores place as 'space plus time', asking us to look beyond the here and now to children's lived experiences of other times, spaces and discourses. After introducing this perspective, the author considers the significance of such spatio-temporality for the facilitation of place connectedness in outdoor learning. The notion of social topology is drawn upon as a way of mapping complex socio-material connections which produce children's relationship with place and influence their activity within outdoor places. An example social topology is provided, drawing on ethnographic data from a wider study of teachers' practices which included time each week in a school 'forest'. The chapter ends with practical ideas for practitioners and researchers to consider in exploring place connection in this way.

In their introduction to *Encountering Ideas of Place in Education*, Rawlings Smith and Pike (2024) remind us that 'place-based learning is a powerful pedagogical approach that connects learning with the physical place in which it happens and seeks to connect learners with the local context' (p. 3). The edited volume draws together a wide variety of examples of place-based learning, woven with a strong theme of place connection. Place is considered in light of how people experience, conceptualise and use physical spaces, through how they relate to themselves, others and the materiality of each space. This conceptualisation of place and place connection is continued in what follows here, building also on the theoretical perspective introduced in Chapter 1 of our book. Within is an argument for greater consideration of the complexities of time and space in understanding what we mean by place, and a way to 'see' such complexities using a social topological lens. Parts of this chapter have been published in the *European Educational Research Journal (EERJ)* (Unsworth, 2024); they are reproduced here with the aim of further articulating how an alternative view of place's space-time can help teachers plan for meaningful *world-self-others* connection during outdoor learning.

Place as Space Plus Time

Place is central to our lived experience. Rather than a passive physical site of activity, place can be seen as an active mediator of (inter)action, sense-making and affective attachment. In education, places can mediate learning, both in students' reaction to place and in what places offer to each educational opportunity. Planning for any educational activity should include, or perhaps begin with, deep consideration of students' possible responses to the place(s) in which this activity is based. Arguments for the importance of considering response to place range from a need for students to feel at ease in their environment in order to participate, to place connection as prime element of the educational experience: 'We could say, the *relationship* between the person and the natural world is the teacher' (Cree & Robb, 2021, n.p., original emphasis). In this sense, place itself 'has much to teach us' (Vander Ark et al., 2020, p. xii).

When we speak of *place* in relation to education, we often talk of *space* and *time* in the here-and-now. Physical sites provide the 'here': school buildings, classrooms, halls. Playgrounds, museums, forests. Residential centres, homes, hillsides. These *spaces* are caught up in *time* too in the sense of the 'now': timetabling, inside/outside classroom routines, time pressures, freedoms, constraints. Spatio-temporal dimensions can support or hinder student engagement in educational activity (see, e.g.

the different perspectives presented in Rawlings Smith and Pike (2024)). This is particularly significant when planning education outside of familiar classroom space-time, and even more so when this is in places of nature, which may not be part of all children's daily lives. Physical spaces in nature, by accident or design, may be very different to those which situate students' wider educational and life experiences. Patterns of time (length of sessions, routines, travelling times) are likely to differ to those experienced in classroom-based education. For many children and young people, such spatiotemporal differences offer breathing space which provides healthy contrast to what is often perceived as performatively-driven classroom-based education, whose spatio-temporality generates identities, behaviours and hierarchical power relations designed to re-produce 'good' test results (Cudworth, 2018). For others, spaces and time-patterns beyond student experience may form barriers to engaging with activity therein, through unfamiliarity and disconnection (Pyle, 2003).

However, harnessing place for educational purposes (whatever these might be) is not simply a matter of considering differences in the here-and-now of classroom versus outdoor places. Spatiotemporal elements of place are wrapped up in *other* spaces and *other* times. Challenges teachers encounter in building students' capacity for place connection may be attitudinal, built up through conversations and experiences of 'the outdoors' outside of school. Students are wrapped up in beliefs about, and cultural positioning of, outdoor spaces (generated over time) in the societies they are part of or interact with. These other spaces and other times may engender positive or resistant attitudes to the outdoor place teachers have chosen (or curated) as the context for educational activity (Clements, 2004; Johansson, 2006).

Consideration of how social activity and cultural trends extend what is meant by place and place connection takes us beyond taken-for-granted locales and moments-in-time (Appadurai, 1988; Rodman, 1992). Place is reimagined as a pause in the continuous flow of the social world (Price, 2013), as both a representation of, and engendering, cultural ways of being (Bourdieu, 1984). Place is 'no longer a category of fixed ontological attributes, but a becoming, an emergent property of social relationships' (Jimenez, 2003, p. 140). The evolution of what we perceive and encounter as 'a place' is complexly social and psychological, formed through association and interpretation within ongoing cumulation of lived experience. Place is more than a location in time – it is also an (individually and socially) imagined place (Anderson, 2021).

Place *connection* is, therefore, more than time spent within a location. It is also the development of a 'sense' of place by *responding* to it. Places are experienced and imagined (Anderson, 2021). They are responded to not only in an immediate physical and temporal experience but also metaphysically. Places are full of associations to other direct experiences (of forests, of fires, of wearing wellies) or indirect experiences (conversations about mud, walking forests as a computer game character) (Unsworth, 2024). How we respond to place(s) involves an affective attachment (Agnew, 1987), generated through material and metaphysical triggers in immediate space-time which connect to internalised and imaginary experience drawn from (fragments of) other space-times. For, episodes in lived experience are not necessarily remembered in their entirety, or even directly present within the educational activity at hand. What may be brought to mind in the here-and-now includes 'metaphors, ideology, and language, as well as behaviors [sic], habits, skills, and spatial orientations derived from global discourses and faraway places' (Low, 2009, p. 34). What influences place response, and the (dis)connections we form through our response, is multifarious and fragmentary, (simultaneously) including that which is present and lingering 'traces' of other space-times. Put simply, the here-and-now also contains 'then' and 'there'; the past in the present matters to experience of, connection to and (re)generation of place (Munn, 1992).

Subsequently, place-responsive pedagogy is more than simply 'using the local community and environment as a starting point to teach concepts' (Sobel, 2004, p. 7). It is about planning for real-world encounters with places that have often already been given a 'sense' of place, materiality and connotative powers over time, in relation to other spaces and other times (see Chapter 3). In this sense, being *place-responsive* pertains to both the planned educational encounter of/within a particular place *and* the embodied lived experiences that students, teachers, sites, materials, weather, clothing (and so on and so forth) will bring into the encounter.

Using Social Topology to Plan for Place-responsive Pedagogy

To teach in a place-responsive way, we must first try to gain a view of the social processes by which places are constructed (Harvey, 1996): the 'common' sense of the place that has been established and students' pre-positioning towards it. To achieve this view, it is useful to consider place and place connection as topological in nature (Bourdieu, 1985): place is produced by, and recursively productive of, a set of related (social and spatiotemporal) positions taken up by its many constituent human and non-human actors. To come back to Akram's (2023) interpretation of Bourdieu's *habitus* (see Chapter 1, Fig. 1.2), relationships between the components of a place together effect (bring into being) a sense of place and how we connect to it. To grasp the complex combinations of 'actors' which produce a sense of place and effect place response, we may employ a *social topological* lens (Decuypere et al., 2022): 'social topology explains times and spaces as relational, dynamic, and continuously unfolding yet, at the same time, as manifesting in powerful agential forms' (p. 872). The notion of topology offers a way to talk of and 'map' Akram's components of place and place connection; to view the ways that place is dynamically distributed across people and things, ideas and attitudes, spaces and times.

Social topology can be used to explore place as constituted and contingent; as a temporary combination of physical entities and interpretative (inter)action. Descriptions can be generated of how physical spaces are imbued with a sense of place and how this is continued/rejected; how interpretation of place reimagines again and again the 'real' of that place: 'there is always a necessary distance between fantasmatic and "real" spacetimes' (Saari, 2022, p. 894). Our main concern becomes that of exploring by what social (interactional, experiential, imagined) processes places are constructed (Harvey, 1996) in a way that encapsulates characteristics shaping common understanding *and* individual (de)formations of place (into something personally significant). Through such efforts, we may deepen our knowledge of the actors at work in place connection/disconnection. We may seek to interrupt, displace, enhance or deepen these connections through adaptation of different components.

Mol and Law (1994) offer useful vocabulary in approaching a social topological perspective of place. The 'social' is seen as not existent in one singular space or time, but rather 'performs itself in a recursive and topologically heterogeneous manner' (p. 641). To describe a place and place connection, we can look to the associations between socio-material actors which constitute our sense of a place. Mol and Law ask us to seek *clusters* of objects, people and ideas which associate repeatedly so that (physical/metaphysical/spatiotemporal) *boundaries* appear. *Networks* form, 'in which distance is a function of relations between elements and difference a matter of relational variety' (p. 641). Space and time bend and weave away from the physical and chronological, refocused as the ways in which actors relate to one another within and across spaces and times. Mol and Law argue a further element of social space, that of *fluid spatiality*: aspects of place which 'are neither delineated by boundaries, nor linked through stable relations: instead, entities may be similar and dissimilar at different locations within fluid space' (p. 641). In the following example of a school 'forest' as a place for/of education, Mol and Law's approach provides a framework by which to make sense of ethnographic data.

Ethnography is a useful methodological approach to gaining a view of the relationship between heterogeneous actors which currently produce places and place connection. Whilst much ethnography runs to longer timescales, many researchers of education draw on ethnographic methods in short-term studies to gain a detailed view of lived experience (Plum, 2018; Unsworth, 2024). This is particularly pertinent to the study of place-responsive education, in which educational encounters are examined as they occur in different spaces and times. An immersive ethnographic approach enables rich description of the here-and-now experience of place, whilst affording opportunity to interrogate (through a suite of observational, discursive and documentary methods) the entanglements of people, materials, ideas and ideals that effect place and place connection. In the example topology below, for instance, I sat amongst the trees with my notebook, observing and occasionally participating in educational life. I made sketches of the physical environment and how teachers and students moved and interacted with(in) these. As I wrote, teachers and students often asked about my notes, which I would share; this led to the sharing of ideas or emotion, clarification of action or pointing to texts, materials, and other people/experiences to observe. Fieldnotes formed the basis of semi-structured interviews ($n = 12$) and documentary tracing ($n = 86$), following the threads of 'trace' actors noted in observations.

The data and findings presented in the example topology (below) are taken from, and discussed more widely in, a paper presented at the Oxford Ethnography in Education Conference in 2023 and later published in the European Educational Research Journal (Unsworth, 2024). In the latter paper can be found the ethnographic 'story' of children's experiences of the forest. Below is presented a topological view of place connection which emerged from this data, with short extracts from the paper's longer vignette included to illustrate each point. This social topological approach can be taken up and used by practitioners in planning and preparing for outdoor learning, and there are questions to support with this at the end of the chapter.

An Example Topology

The following example is part of a wider ethnographic study of teachers' practices in an English primary school which involved weekly time in the school 'forest'. The school is large (three-form entry) and set within a varied socio-economic context that includes both higher and lower income families. The school has worked hard towards opening spaces in the school day for children to learn outdoors. Three teachers from the school (at the time of the study) were trained in the 'Forest School' approach advocated by the Forest School Association (FSA) (see Chapter 6). This training was not used at this school to provide a 'set' approach to learning outdoors but rather contributed to the development of whole-school principles around outdoor learning: time and space to explore interests, to use and ponder taught skills/knowledge, to be in and with nature, to observe, experience, notice the world. In this sense, the term 'Forest School' as applied in the example below refers to localised interpretation and practices, rather than the FSA-accredited approach.

Forest School sessions relied on an open-ended pedagogy, with individual and interpersonal connection with natural and teacher-supplied resources left largely open to children's interests and imaginations. Teachers were empowered by school leaders to follow principles of outdoor learning derived from FSA training but not limited to these. Principles were discussed and left open-ended. Aside from centralised health and safety policy (risk assessments of outdoor learning on the premises and relating to use of specific forest equipment such as whittling equipment), the forest could be used as a space to work with children on aspects of their education deemed important by the teachers. Some teacher-directed tasks focussed on historical–cultural uses of natural artefacts, such as stick whittling, but these too maintained much of the character of play, in that children could take up the skills (within health and safety parameters instructed by the teacher) in ways that suited their own ideas and uses. The role of teachers in the forest was to encourage and extend children's interests and play. Teachers listened and observed. Children's individual or collective interactions with the forest sparked moments of interjection (to ask, e.g. 'If you're interested in… have you seen…?' or to subtly offer further resources to incorporate into play). The ways that children interacted with and within the forest was sometimes similar to other children, but more commonly was individualised.

Patterns in forest interactions were identified through iterative-inductive coding of observations, interview data and documents pertaining to immediate/trace actors. Coding was used to map the topology of the forest: actor associations generative of place and place connection (see Fig. 4.1):

Building Connection to Place • 93

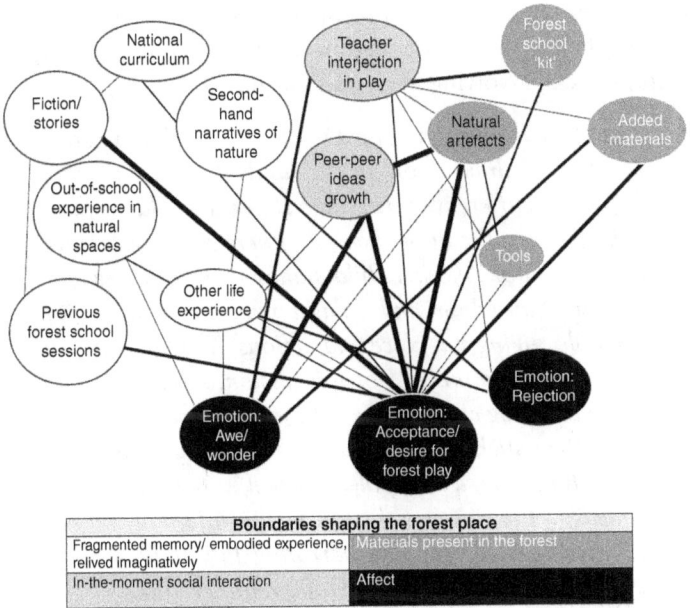

Fig. 4.1. A Topology of a School 'Forest' as Educational Place.

Data were analysed in terms of clusters of actors which signalled 'boundaries' in the sense-making of the forest place: fragmented memory/embodied experience, relived imaginatively; materials present in the forest; affect; in-the-moment social interaction. Key actors within these 'boundaries' are shown in the different shading used in Fig. 4.1. Network relations between boundaried elements of the forest are represented by weighted lines (the thicker the line, the more frequent the association). Aspects of the forest which maintained fluid spatiality are highlighted through ethnographic description of differences in activity within boundary elements.

Boundaries/Clusters

Children largely connect to the forest via fragmented memories (embodied experiences relived imaginatively), spurred by in-the-moment interaction and response to materiality, and productive of affect. In Akram's (2023) terms, their place connection involves embodiment of meaning derived from other times and spaces which effects unconscious positioning towards the forest. The boundaries of the forest, in this school, are largely metaphysical, involving ideas and imagination:

> *The class disperses amongst the trees...[children] work together to draw doors in the sand: 'Mine's a portal', one says. Different stories take shape as children play, some leaving the doors behind, others centring around a chosen door. Another child makes a hole in a tree into her own 'fairy door' and walks a pinecone in and out of the hole, giving it a voice and actions in an impromptu story. Towards the end of the session, six children sit around the log circle and whittle, quietly chatting about what their stick is going to be (a mast for a pirate ship, a jousting pole, a tent pole, a pencil). One giggles and squeaks, 'I'm not a stick! I'm Stickman!', dancing her stick in front of her and parroting Julia Donaldson's book 'Stickman' (Unsworth, 2024, pp. 10–11).*

The forest became a place of fiction and storytelling, through stories experienced elsewhere now fragmented into remembrances. These stories act as catalysts to the evocation of meaning relating to the materiality of the forest. But they rely upon the pedagogical approach of openness and exploration which allows children freedom to take for granted that the artefacts of the forest may become anything at all besides what they actually are (sticks, leaves, shadows).

Embodied attitudes to nature provide metaphysical boundaries also tied to the relationship between materiality and memory. An encounter with mud sparked secondary perceptions of nature:

> 'What's up?' Alex [the class teacher] asks.
>
> *The child shrugs and says,* 'It's dirty in there, I got mucky'.
>
> 'You don't like the soil?'
>
> *The child shakes his head.* 'It's not good to play in the dirt. I have to keep clean' (Unsworth, 2024, p. 10)

A heard discourse of 'mud is bad' positions a child against the place, generating a sense of non-belonging to be overcome. Conversely, other children gladly interact with and within the forest; for some, natural artefacts sparked episodic memories of other out-of-school times in the outdoors (fire-building, camping, or playing with friends in the countryside).

It is clear that material–memory relationality is important to the shaping of forest boundaries. In the brief examples above, connections to the forest are forged through the ways that natural and manmade artefacts mediate children's ideas and actions by sparking connections to other (immediate/trace) actors in different spaces and/or times. This is an interior–exterior encounter, and therefore, *both* internal and external 'worlds' need to be taken into consideration. Whilst some of these repeated connections are unprompted and naturally emergent from the combination of place and person, teachers intentionally design the forest experience to spark children's connections to the world. Critical pedagogies of place afford a view of such moves as a curation of place in relation to education: a place becomes *educational* through its (re)constitution as spatial aspects of social experience (Gruenewald, 2003), created and continued by connected social actors which determine students' engagement (Smyth, Angus, et al., 2008).

In this sense, one consideration for educators lies in how they might curate outdoor spaces in ways which spark association with children's lived experiences: with stories, discussions, curriculum, social and emotional wellbeing. This could fruitfully include consideration of how associations might be generated which *challenge* children's current perceptions and experience, extending their conceptualisation of the world. Creating opportunities for associative connection in outdoor places does not have to be obvious or direct (e.g. a book brought outdoors) but can be subtle: a suggestion. A pile of sticks, perhaps, if children have enjoyed Julia Donaldson's *Stickman* story, or some gardening equipment if they have asked questions about how plants grow. In this way, the child may forge their own associations and choose to explore them, opening potential for deepening thought about the world. Place, in this sense, is (through the teacher's curation) taking on the pedagogical imperative of 'pointing' (Biesta, 2021), facilitating children in noticing the world, in forging connections, in exploring ideas (rather than directing or transmitting knowledge).

It is also important to note that children come to the forest having already experienced nature and natural places. If they have not directly experienced natural places, children may have encountered ideas, beliefs and attitudes associated with nature through conversation, books and computer games. It is also through pre-attitudinal positioning that children make sense of the forest, along with accompanying affective response. Some children will readily accept the place and feel happy, confident or excited to be within it. Others reject and disconnect. (Dis)connection viewed topologically affords further argument for reconsidering commercialised versions of education in forest places and recognition rather of 'how Forest School as a form of outdoor education is culturally, socially and historically situated' (Leather, 2018, p. 5). It is important for teachers to consider current structural barriers to outdoor learning, be that a metaphysical barrier of an idea of mud (which is picked up in Chapter 5 by Tracy Hayes), or a physical barrier relating to a particular learning need (such as is a consideration by Lucy Sors in Chapter 3). The boundaries and actor associations noted through a social topological approach can support in 'seeing' areas where place connection can be strengthened or disconnection transformed.

Network Associations

To overcome disconnection with the forest place in the extract provided above, teachers forge connections between material 'kit' – wellies, puddlesuits – that signal a way of connecting with the forest in a way that also aligns with pre-existing attitudinal positions towards mud:

> Alex nods and pauses. 'You've got wellies on though. They protect your trousers. So, you could go and balance on the log you liked last time if you like and your clothes will stay clean'.
>
> 'Last time I had a puddlesuit on'.

> Alex smiles. 'Shall we go and get you one on then?'. The child agrees. Alex helps him to don a puddlesuit and the child runs off into the forest, climbing and balancing on logs (Unsworth, 2024, p. 11).

The ways that teachers anticipate the need for this kit, despite the fair weather, suggest their consideration of students' attitudes towards the forest and what is needed to break down place connection barriers for different children. Connections are forged to materiality in 'real' time but also in forging connections between different forest sessions: we did this last time and the time before, shall we do this now? These connections support children in finding their own way to respond to the forest place and are an important consideration for teachers in planning place connection experiences *over time*.

Similarly, metaphysical boundaries are furrowed through repeated ways in which teachers and children use the materials of the forest. Teachers repeatedly offer a pedagogy of free play through freedom of association in what the forest signifies to each person:

> Later, I will ask Alex about this approach, and he will tell me that, 'It's about giving them freedom to think. So, the forest means something different to each of them. It might mean something different next week too. I look for opportunities to join in or point something out' (Unsworth, 2024, p. 10).

One teacher calls this 'offering interesting things for children to connect with'. Children remind each other of games played in previous sessions that they wish to continue (and materials added by teachers, such as fairy doors and whittle sticks). Repetition helps create a sense of *this* forest place, which is a place of world-exploration and open-ended play. One area of the forest which provides repeated encounters with aspects of the world is a garden area:

> Two children wander to a gardened area with the beginnings of shoots poking up from a recently dug earth. 'They're growing! They're growing!' one child excitedly reports to their friend. Alex wanders

> over and chats to them, asking them why they think these plants have grown so quickly (Unsworth, 2024, p. 10).

Children visit and revisit this area, planting, watching for change. This is the beauty of *slow* pedagogy and the (literal, in some seasons) fruitfulness of repeated and extended time in places of nature advocated by Clark (2021). Repeated connective possibilities can be mapped across planned provision for outdoor learning; forged connections noted and continued, returned to, or expanded in ongoing provision of outdoor learning experiences.

It is also worth noting that the repetitions which define the boundaries of education in this forest rely upon social relations. Teachers work together to agree a place-responsive pedagogical approach that allows for open-ended connections and extensions of thought. Students play together, reminding each other of previous uses of the forest. Place emerges, then, from an entanglement of natural/teacher-curated materiality and social interaction. In turn, children begin to 'see themselves' within these connections (Cudworth & Lumber, 2021, p. 73), overcoming strong emotional reactions to participate in activity, finding preferred ways to engage with the forest. It is a worlding, a togethering, as well as a 'selfing' of place. This is a development of the individual subject/subject in common with others (Ingold, 2017), which sits aside from the imperative of qualification which runs throughout much curriculum work (Biesta, 2021). There are few pre-defined outcomes in this approach aside from a sense of world-self-others connection.

Fluid Spatiality

Teachers' intentional design and usage of the forest space throws wide the forest as a blank canvas on which children may daub their own interpretative colours. There is an open-endedness to the signification of natural and man-made objects which engenders children's individual playful communion with forest materiality. Little doors, whittlesticks, shadows, leaves do not have clear pre-established relationships between themselves (nor to education) and this ambiguity is continued in the way that they are introduced (safe handling of tools and a quick history of whittling aside). The stuff of the forest calls to children:

> *Three children hop from shadow to shadow, cast by the high sun on waving trees. Two put their hands in and out of light patches: 'We're catching the sunshine', they tell me (Unsworth, 2024, p. 11).*

Children notice and use the forest: trees, light, shadows, teacher-made objects, are all left to work their own mediation of playful activity. This is perhaps a stark contrast to ways of being and knowing in the classroom; an escape from an era of performativity and marketisation of education (Ball, 2008). The latter has been explored as reducing children's individual autonomy of thought and action: 'the pressures and potential disadvantages that accountability can bring... Asking for help becomes the norm, rather than an approach which empowers students to take responsibility for their own learning' (Edgington, 2016, p. 309). Teachers do not use forest sessions strictly in the service of the national curriculum, rather as a 'space set apart... removed from the physical constraints of the classroom and pedagogical constraints of the national curriculum' (Harris, 2018, p. 222).

The overarching fluidity of the forest place – which is made sense of differently by different children – allows children to forge an affective connection to which teachers can then respond. Disconnection becomes evident quickly and is equally quickly addressed. Connections to literature, science, or other imaginative play (to the various inner worlds of children) are observed and built upon, taking individual place sense-making to different senses of this place, or to provoke deeper thinking about aspects of the world children encounter in and through the forest. Whilst there are clear limitations of a 'badge required' Forest School approach (see Louise Hawxwell and Nicky Bolton's discussion in Chapter 6), if taken more 'loosely', the values underpinning much Forest School training (of freer, playful pedagogy) remain pertinent for place-responsive pedagogy in outdoor learning: 'Through its emphasis on free play and exploration, it [Forest School] creates a unique space to foster relational and meaning-making opportunities within the natural environment' (Cudworth & Lumber, 2021, p. 80). At this school, such values exhibit in teaching structured around fluidity of place and place connection. This is education done differently; conversationally and responsively, with place the thing that it is 'put on the table' for discussion and response. Both place and teacher are, in this sense, in role as 'pointer' to interesting/puzzling things in the world (Biesta, 2021).

Concluding Remarks

Employing a social topological lens, we may see more clearly how a *sense of place* and *place connection* are forged. Place is neither spatially nor temporally static, but rather caught up in flows of meaning, mobilities of thought and materiality, and connectivity between social actors (Lingard, 2022). Teachers may wish to take a deeper look at the places within which they are situating their pedagogy. They may wish to draw on ethnographic methods to 'deep hang out' (Geertz, 1998) in the spaces they provide for children to connect with 'the outdoors' and to generate, through this approach, a rich description of how that place is currently positioned/interpreted within the social group. Educators may wish to explore how current embodied lived experience may be harnessed/may be a barrier to the connection that children will form with(in) each place.

An expanded notion of time and space in concepts of place supports us in better understanding and planning for place-responsive pedagogy. We may see how relationships between materiality and memory matter to how *all* children can be included in outdoor learning. Not all children come to opportunities to learn outside the classroom with prior experience of that place, particularly in relation to nature. This in turn establishes different initial responses and connections which need time for expression and discussion, for teacher and student response. Echoing the urgency of slow as advocated by Clark (2022), this calls for pedagogy centred around lived experience and connection to world (Biesta, 2021). The particular case presented in this chapter extends these educational movements, offering food for thought around the constituency and contingencies of the 'place(s)' of education: how places might be curated to engender unhurried connection, and to act as 'pointer' to possible responsive encounters between the world, the self and others.

To approach place-responsive pedagogy through a social topological lens:

- Engage students in deep thinking about the place they are in. After being in the place, ask them to draw a 'map' of it by drawing the things they played there. They can choose how to represent each game or thing that stood out to them.
- Observe children during free play in that place: What are they drawn to? What influences their play?
- Use the maps and your observations to develop a topology of the forest place for use in planning for place connection and place-responsive pedagogy. Map the social topology of the forest (or other place) in terms of how children currently understand it (such as in Fig. 4.1).
- Sort the influences you observe into direct stimulus (artefacts/social interaction within the forest space) and indirect, or trace, influences (stories, second-hand narratives of nature, experiences of other natural spaces). Is there a dominant influence shaping what each place means to particular children/groups/the class as a whole?
- Notice barriers to engagement with the place. What would help overcome these barriers? (see, e.g. Chapter 3).

CHAPTER 5

Mudfulness? Nurturing a Relationship with Nature Through Serendipitous Encounters with Mud

Tracy Ann Hayes

Plymouth Marjon University, UK

ABSTRACT

Through reflection on more than two decades of environmental practice and educational research, this chapter draws on autoethnographic techniques to creatively explore young people's relationship to nature. The playful concept of mudfulness is introduced as offering potential to develop relationships through serendipitous encounters with mud – through practical activities or playful adventures outside. The chapter reviews existing research on mud play's sensory appeal and benefits, highlighting its physical, psychological, and emotional advantages for children. However, it identifies a research gap concerning young people (11+). Two stories of 'muddy moments' involving young people, practitioners, and researchers are shared and interpreted to address this gap. This illustrates the therapeutic and educational benefits of serendipitous encounters with mud, and how this may contribute to nurturing a positive relationship with nature. The chapter closes with final reflections on the importance of muddy play, whatever our biological age.

Introduction

A well-known song exhorts the glorious nature of mud and its potential benefits for health and well-being by cooling the blood (Flanders & Swann, 1957). I urge caution in seeking it out, as many consider it an earworm – a tune that gets stuck in your head, lingering in your mind, sometimes for hours or even days. Typically, earworms are harmless; however, they can be annoying when you cannot stop thinking about them. This is similar to some memories from my research and practice over the last two decades. There are 'magic moments' (Bacharach & David, 1957 – another potential earworm) that are often small and seemingly unimportant, yet have lingered in my memory, sparked my curiosity and provoked me to pause and analyse their meaning (Hayes & Prince, 2019). I do that in this chapter as I reflect on some *muddy moments* with young people – playfully conceptualised as 'mudfulness' – that arose through serendipitous encounters with mud. Serendipity refers to the occurrence of events by chance in a happy or beneficial way, encapsulating the experience of accidentally discovering something pleasant or valuable without actively seeking it. It is a term that originates in the mid-18th century with the writer Horace Walpole, who was inspired by a Persian fairy tale called 'The Three Princes of Serendip' (Colman, 2006). Serendipitous experiences and observations lie behind the apparent genius of many great discoveries. As physicist Joseph Henry states, 'the seeds of great discoveries are constantly floating around us, but they only take root in minds well prepared to receive them' (cited in Colman, 2006, p. 161). Like tilling the soil (mud) to enable plants to grow, minds need to be receptive and responsive to make the most of serendipitous moments.

The whimsical manner in which I open this chapter captures the essence of my research into young people's relationships with nature, which argues for more playful approaches to outdoor learning (OL) for young people that allow for spontaneity, creativity, and responsiveness – to people and environments around us – enabling opportunities for young people (older children) to play and have fun (Hayes, 2017a). This is important because Westernised countries define or categorise people based on the age of their physical bodies (Valentine et al., 1998,

p. 2), accompanied by inherent societal and cultural expectations of age-appropriate behaviour – which defines what is in/acceptable in different situations. As a result, the world becomes much more serious around the age of 11–13 (coinciding with puberty for most young people), with the UK educational focus shifting from playful stories and environmental awareness-raising to learning about citizenship and environmental stewardship. Young people are encouraged to become more responsible (Hayes, 2015). I have long questioned if this shift lies behind the apparent disconnection that many young people may have with nature – does (over)burdening young people with environmental issues result in them becoming disenchanted with nature? – especially at a stage in their lives (adolescence) when they face so many other challenges. I have also argued for using playful methods when researching and discussing play and playfulness. I do not believe people can be too old or 'seriously academic' to play. I use this chapter to demonstrate how serious points can be made in a way that embraces imagination, recognises the value of serendipity and spontaneity, and ultimately emphasises the need to provide opportunities to be creative and have fun, which brings health and well-being benefits for people and the environment.

Mud, often overlooked as unremarkable or seen as messy, dirty and inconvenient, holds significant potential for fostering positive relationships with nature and promoting overall well-being. Drawing from autoethnographical reflections on empirical and anecdotal evidence, I make a case for embracing serendipitous encounters with mud. I identify a need to look critically at the opportunities we offer young people to be outside – to allow more time and space for *being* outdoors, as well as *doing* outdoors, and to have fun beyond traditional conservation, education and sporting activities. Elsewhere, I have argued for kindness (Hayes, 2017b; Hayes et al., 2021), playfulness (Hayes, 2015; Hayes & Murphy, 2022; Hayes & Tremble, 2022) and inclusive practice (Hayes, 2020/2016). I add to that here with 'mudfulness' – the potential to develop positive relationships with nature through serendipitous encounters with mud. My use of 'mudfulness' aims to embrace the complexities and controversies of encountering mud, ranging from aversion to delight (and everything in between). Mud has a sensory appeal – the smell of it, the feel of it, the sight of it, and the noise it makes when we engage with it in its wet forms. The onomatopoeic words we use to describe it hint at the fun of interacting with it. However, for some, it may be seen as dirty, dangerous, and smelly – something to be avoided (Parsons & Traunter, 2019). Most notably, a recent campaign by Persil promoted that 'Dirt is Good. Play On!... dirt is part of the game' (Unilever, 2024), highlighting the power of its products to remove stains. Muddy encounters, when humans meet mud – feet slipping in it, hands covered in it, the impact of an unplanned slide – offer opportunities for fun and learning. What may at first appear to be a simple encounter can become a more embodied, entangled experience. Unlike mindfulness, I do not propose mudfulness as an academic concept or suggest a structured way of embracing it; it is merely a playful way to draw attention to an element of the natural environment encountered in everyday life.

Through an overview of research into the human–nature relationship, I acknowledge the varied definitions and perceptions of 'nature' and the importance of recognising the multifaceted ways people interact with the natural environment. Then, I review the literature on the restorative powers of direct contact with nature for children and highlight the physical, psychological, and emotional benefits of messy, muddy outdoor play. While muddy play is commonly associated with early childhood, I argue that its benefits extend to adolescents and adults, suggesting that such experiences promote spontaneity, creativity, and a sense of connection with the natural world. The chapter includes two small stories illustrating the transformative potential for adolescents of spontaneously engaging with mud. These stories highlight the joy and relational aspects of muddy play. The chapter concludes by advocating for more research into the benefits of muddy play for adolescents – emphasising the need for playful, creative approaches in both practice and research related to nature engagement.

Review of Literature

Nature is a small, rather vague word. It is a 'common notion, which everyone is familiar with as long as we are not asked to define it' (Ducarme, 2021, p. 1). However, it is important to recognise that 'nature' is highly contested with many different definitions; indeed, even the use of it in the conventional singular form is contentious. As Taylor argues, it may represent a romanticised, 'seductive' view and she suggests an alternative, reconstructed 'natureculture common worlds' (Taylor, 2013, p. 115) that embraces plural natures. However, consciously choosing to use the conventional singular form shifts the focus from an academic, philosophical/theoretical one to more of an everyday, practical one that can reach a more diverse audience. An everyday definition of nature as the physical world and everything in it (such as plants, animals, mountains, and stars) that is not made by people, as well as the natural forces that control what happens in the world. This does not ignore that much of what is considered a 'natural environment' is manufactured, moulded, and manipulated by humans, nor that we are indeed nature. The defining feature of places we identify as natural is how they are perceived and experienced by the people using them.

Parents, teachers, youth and community workers, and other adults have an important role in young people's access to and use of outdoor spaces (Parsons & Traunter, 2020); therefore, it is essential that they pause and consider their own relationship with nature and be aware of how their perceptions impact the way they support (or not) others. Kellert outlines different ways of categorising experiences of nature, including representational experiences of nature, for example, through stories and toys (typically in the early years), computers or images; indirect experiences, such as structured/facilitated contact with 'managed' nature that 'requires ongoing human input for its survival, like a garden, a potted plant, or a pet' (Kellert in Dunlap & Kellert, 2012, p. 133); and direct experience, for example, unstructured play and contact with wild places, self-sustaining nature (typically in youth). I disagree with Kellert's identification of gardening as an indirect experience – managed nature may not be the same as 'wild nature', but it still provides opportunities for young people to have direct engagement, embodied experiences, a chance to get muddy hands, handle worms (and other wildlife), see and feel the changing seasons. Not everyone can access genuinely wild places – if indeed, there are any, considering the global impact of humans – to directly experience nature, and gardens and farms provide many therapeutic and educational benefits for young people (Hayes et al., 2022).

There is a wealth of literature on the restorative powers and health benefits of direct contact with nature, including mental, physical, and social well-being (e.g. Hartig et al., 1991; Kaplan, 1995; Skar et al., 2016a; Ulrich, 1984). It is generally accepted that early experiences in nature are important for developing an awareness of and a connection to nature (see, e.g. Chawla, 1990; Dunlap & Kellert, 2012; Waite, 2007). A growing body of research into children's need to play outdoors suggests that it provides many physical, psychological, and emotional benefits for children (Davis & Elliott, 2004; Hayes & Leather, 2020; Hayes et al., 2021; Mainstone-Cotton, 2017; Parsons & Traunter, 2020), as well as being a fun, playful way of encouraging a positive relationship with nature. Mainstone-Cotton (2017) highlights the importance of sensory play, using loose parts such as mud, sticks, and leaves, as a way of helping to promote young children's emotional health and well-being. More than a decade earlier, Davis and Elliott had similarly argued that 'direct experiences with the natural environment are also important for sensory development' (Davis & Elliott, 2004, p. 2).

While some studies may focus on these benefits within early years education, others (me included) extend this focus to young adulthood – and beyond. Fruin, an outdoor educator with experience in the UK and Australia defines muddy play as 'any form of playing outdoors that directly involves mud, such as mixing soil and water to make mud cakes or squelching feet in a muddy puddle' (Fruin, 2020, p. 69). Mud-making activities (see Somerville & Powell, 2019) are more likely to be purposefully undertaken by young children than adolescents, for whom it tends to be more spontaneous. Outdoor play also indirectly involves getting muddy – digging for worms or exploring a muddy woodland area. While there might not be as extensive literature on muddy play with adolescents or adults compared to that with children, there are researchers and authors who have explored the broader concept of outdoor play, including activities like mud play, among older age groups. Much outdoor education and environmental sustainability research explores the benefits of nature-based experiences and examines how outdoor activities, including those involving natural materials like mud, can promote well-being and environmental stewardship among young people and adults (e.g. Gray & Thomson, 2016; Truong et al., 2016). Richard Louv (2011), known primarily for his work around addressing nature-deficit disorder in children, has written extensively about the importance of nature across the lifespan, including the benefits of nature experiences for adults, including activities like gardening, hiking, and outdoor recreation, which could involve muddy play.

Muddy play is a relatively new phenomenon, which can be linked to a corresponding rise in the popularity of forest schools (see FSA, 2025) and a focus on evidencing the importance of OL (see IOL, 2024). In 2011, Liz Edwards and Jan White, under the organisational name of *Muddy Faces*, launched a 'Mud Campaign' to highlight the importance of allowing young children to play with natural resources – especially mud (hence the name). Their research indicated that only a few early years settings were taking this approach, and they determined to change this by providing a wealth of information on mud, with practical guidance and activities for practitioners and parents, together with a repository of relevant research articles. In the UK, most early years settings and many primary schools now contain a mud kitchen and encourage muddy play activities. To support this practice, numerous books and websites offer practical guidance and fun activities, such as *20 glorious ways to play with mud!* (Whitehouse, 2017).

Making pies from mud is nothing new – the first children on earth likely engaged in this simple, natural, playful activity by scooping up mud between their fingers to mix with water from nearby puddles, mimicking the more focussed activities of adults around them who were forming the mud (clay) into useful objects such as pots and bowls. Somerville and Powell (2019), when researching for their paper on *Thinking posthuman with mud: and children of the Anthropocene*, found that mud:

> ... *has its own websites, definitions, languages, rituals and traditions.* Mud is defined as a mixture of water and any combination of different kinds of soil loam, silt and clay.

> *Ceremonial ochres are made of mud and mud provides a home for worms, frogs, snails, clams, crayfish, larva and various insects. The word* mud *is found in various forms of ancient languages... (p. 831, original emphasis).*

However, playful approaches to mud do not generally extend beyond early childhood. By the time children reach their pre-teens, their contact with mud generally becomes limited to physical education (PE) and games (see Skar et al., 2016a), for example, football, cross-country running, and rugby and the focus shifts from playful play to competitive play, from imagination to determination to succeed, with more intentionality behind activities. Numerous researchers raise concerns that the lives of many children and young people, particularly in the UK and USA, do not allow much space for nature and that contemporary lives tend to be more urban, and indoors-based. This 'extinction of experience' (Pyle, 1993; Soga & Gaston, 2016) is a result of many intersecting factors, including a loss of opportunity to directly experience nature and a loss of positive orientation towards nature, an 'emotional affinity with nature' (Soga & Gaston, 2016, p. 98). The reasons for these losses are complex and varied: increase in urban living and working; more sedentary leisure activities (e.g. computer games, television, using the internet); longer working hours, increased pressures related to formal education; parental concerns, and busier neighbourhoods with more traffic and less safe places for children and young people to play without adult supervision. This may lead to escalating alienation of humanity from the natural world, with resultant 'degradation of public health and wellbeing, loss of emotional affinity to nature, and decline in pro-environmental attitudes and behaviour, implying a cycle of disaffection towards nature' (Soga & Gaston, 2016, p. 94). To counteract this, in recent years, there has been an increasing focus on developing and nurturing young people's connection with nature, and to achieve this, youth work approaches within conservation/environmental organisations have been embraced.

There have also been adventurous, exciting initiatives that aim to attract older young people and adults, for example: 'Tough Mudder' challenges that urge participants to 'Make Your Muddy Miles Count' by raising funds for charitable organisations (Tough

Mudder, n.d.). There are also numerous extreme adventure sports, gardening, leisure activities, conservation, etc. The real gaps in provision come in the 'tween' years – the years between childhood and adulthood. However, many benefits identified for young children can be extended to adolescents. The potential to develop positive relationships with nature through serendipitous encounters with mud was an unexpected discovery – young people (and practitioners) reported feeling good about getting muddy. This was certainly not something I had anticipated. In the following section, the focus of this chapter shifts from literature to lived experience as I reflect on specific 'muddy moments' with young people – time to get muddy!

Muddy Moments with Young People

Before moving into academia, I was a child, family, and youth worker in environmental/conservation. I encountered first-hand the difficulties of encouraging some young people to engage with environmental issues. At practitioner conferences, seminars, and training events related to my role, I heard about adults' concerns for young people's lack of connection with nature, often conceptualised as 'nature-deficit disorder' (Louv, 2009) to be remedied through a healthy dose of 'Vitamin N' (nature) (Louv, 2011) or 'Vitamin G' (green space) (Soga & Gaston, 2016). I also spent time with many young people who loved being outside, were passionate about environmental issues and enjoyed mucking in and helping with practical tasks. Together, we built paths and steps; constructed wildlife-watching hides (badger and birds) and bird and bat boxes; created a bird feeding station and an outdoor 'classroom' from woven willow; coppiced, pruned, lit fires; planted trees and sowed seeds. We got wet, smelled of wood smoke and got very muddy. Arguably, most importantly, we had fun – we incorporated time and space for socialising and spontaneity in what we did. Every practical day included food – bananas baked with giant chocolate buttons; jacket potatoes cooked on the bonfire; barbecued food (of various kinds, including satsumas); hot drinks made using a Kelly Kettle (Jade, 2008) to boil the water, fuelled by dried leaves, twigs, and bits of wood found near where we were working. Preparing and eating the food gave us time to talk, relax, and be together in an outdoor space – and if they wanted to, they could play. The young people I spent time with appeared to have a positive relationship with nature, whatever the weather we encountered. However, I kept hearing and reading about children and young people's lack of connection.

I have researched various facilitated programmes similar to the ones I used to lead that offered OL opportunities for young people (aged 11–25). I have explored young people's perceptions of their experiences and talked with practitioners responsible for designing or delivering the programmes. I have listened to and observed people's stories. Embracing everyday language and drawing on data from numerous naturalistic conversations, anecdotes, and observations, I have created new stories based on these experiences – stories that dwell on small, intimate moments that tend to get lost amongst bigger, less subjective studies (see Hayes & Prince, 2019). Themes revealed through my research highlighted pressures from peers, family, and school to 'grow up' and be responsible, the influence of the facilitator/practitioner, and the importance of kindness, comfort, and a sense of belonging. One of my key findings was that young people (and practitioners) responded most enthusiastically when the facilitator of OL experiences was playful (Hayes, 2015) – and sometimes, this involved mud. To exemplify this, I am sharing two short stories of muddy moments from my doctoral study (Hayes, 2017a; also see Hayes, 2017b, where I reflect on walking with young people as we struggle to cross a muddy field in ill-fitting boots).

Sticks and mud, but thankfully no stones

Tracy: We make the short walk that seems to take hours and safely arrive at the park. Mary[1] has found the walk difficult. She becomes excited at the sight of the mud and puddles. She picks up a stick and starts enthusiastically stirring a muddy puddle as if it is a bowl of porridge. She also stamps in the mud, appearing to enjoy the feel and sound it makes. She looks happy and relaxed. A couple of other girls see what she is doing

---

[1] Mary is the pseudonym for a young woman, aged 13, who has Down's syndrome and attends a specialist secondary school in England for young people with profound and multiple learning disabilities.

and come to join her. Things get a bit livelier – she gets very excited and tries to draw with a muddy stick on one of the other's arms, splattering mud on her coat. There is lots of squealing. Then, she is removed from the area by staff. She doesn't like this and starts picking up and throwing sticks. Thankfully, there are no stones within reach, which could really cause harm. She is clearly angry and frustrated at being removed from the muddy puddles and is taken to one side to recover. She is sat on a bench with a teaching assistant, sullenly watching the others, and defiantly staring at passers-by. An older lady with her grandchild walks by, the toddler stops to look at Mary. The grandmother appears in a hurry and encourages the child to move on. Unhappy at being rushed, the child sits on the ground and begins to cry. Captured by this moment, Mary responds by picking up a stick and walking over to the child. She crouches at eye level, maintains eye contact with the toddler, and hands him her stick. The child instantly stops crying and smiles back at her. He stands up, proudly holding his stick aloft and walks over to his grandmother. I watch, entranced, as he happily walks off with his stick clasped firmly in his hand. Mary sits back down, visibly more relaxed, then spots two dogs with very muddy paws walking past with their owner. She engages the owner in a conversation about the dogs, calmly stroking and talking to them. She is like a different person. The transformation began with mud but took time and space to unfurl. Later, Amy[2] and I reflect on the session. We agree that if we had waterproofs and wellies for all, it wouldn't matter about rain or mud – there would be less chance of young people being told off for splashing or getting dirty. She is going to look into this.

[Story based on my field notes, Hayes 2017]

---

2. The pseudonym for the environmental practitioner who was facilitating the activities that day.

Playing in puddles and mudslides on the lawn

Robert:[3] I was working on a residential at the weekend. There were three boys and one girl, and they all got on really well as a group. It was raining a lot, and it was cold, but the young people loved jumping in the puddles, belly sliding in the mud, actually on their stomachs, and wearing their waterproofs. We'd been on a zip wire, and while some of us were waiting for the others to come down, one of the young people looked around and said, 'I just can't wait to go and jump in some puddles like that one over there'. That young person was afraid of heights. He'd gone up to the platform but didn't come down the zip wire. He was more excited by the puddles than the actual activity. There they were, these 14-, 15- and 17-year-olds, playing like children – belly-sliding across the lawn – and they didn't even stop when another group approached. Some in the other group wanted to join in, but they weren't allowed. It was a combination of the setting, the people, being away from home, away from peer pressure, and being with people who also want to have fun. They did this twice, looking for places for mudslides, but they didn't really talk about it afterwards except to say, 'this has been really great'.

[Account of a recorded conversation with a practitioner, Hayes 2017]

Discussion

The two small stories illustrate that the muddy moments were serendipitous because they were not planned or anticipated. They were unexpected but made possible because there was sufficient time and space for them to occur. Chance was a central feature in their play (Pettersen, 2024, p. 4) as young people responded to the environment around them. I present them first in a non-extrapolated manner to illustrate rather than to tell you what I found. As identified by Ingold: 'the idea of showing is an important one. To show something to

---

3. The pseudonym for the youth development worker.

somebody is to cause it to be seen or otherwise experienced – whether by touch, taste, smell or hearing – by that other person' (Ingold, 2000, p. 21). This approach is advocated by both Pelias (2004, p. 1) as a way of inviting 'identification and empathetic connection' and Sparkes (2007, p. 522), in that in this format, the story 'simply asks for your consideration'. It does not linger on methodology or theoretical concepts, instead leaving it open to the reader's interpretation with the aim of resonance.

However, the stories may be interpreted in various ways, and I will focus on two of them. But, before I do this, I encourage you to pause and consider how you may engage, learn, and reflect on my stories and experience – and your own – and think, as I have done, about how this can be used to enhance your own practice. First, from a practical, pragmatic sense, we can use learning from the stories to identify resources and activities that may be desirable for future, similar occasions, for example, identifying a designated area for mudslides, away from the 'posh lawn'; providing waterproof clothing and footwear, and for developing guidance for practitioners who work with young people outdoors (Hayes et al., 2016). It can be argued that such practical reasoning leads to Mary being removed from the puddles – despite her obvious enjoyment – to prevent her from covering herself or others in yucky, dirty mud. There was no opportunity to explore this with the practitioner or Mary, and I am cautious that an attempt at interpretation may result in inaccurate assumptions. Practitioners have a duty of care to the children they look after and a responsibility for safeguarding the well-being of all. Therefore, it is understandable that they are concerned by the other child's squeals and intervene to maintain control of the situation – especially given the public nature of the park. However, I urge all people in roles like this to pause and consider the impact of their actions (Hayes, 2020).

A second, alternative interpretation inspired by Hackett and Rautio, drawing on more-than-human multimodal meaning-making, perceives these as moments when young people were 'answering the world' when they were 'deeply entwined in a more-than-human world' (Hackett & Rautio, 2019, p. 1019) – a muddy world. From this perspective, Mary and the young people in Robert's story were corresponding with their environment (after Ingold, 2013 cited in Hackett & Rautio, 2019), responding to human and nonhuman actors and answering the world. Young people were 'thinking from their bodies and with the objects and beings that animate them' (Hackett & Rautio, 2019, p. 1024). This resonates more deeply when the children involved, like Mary, have additional support needs and may have had traumatic experiences in education, again, like Mary, whom a previous school described as being 'a devil child'. Caught up in the moment, splashing in the water, flicking mud, holding out a stick to a younger child, stroking a muddy dog, Mary appeared happy in her way of 'answering the world'. 'Answering the world' and responding to the world through muddy encounters links well to *'world centered education'* theories where 'the task of education is to make encounters with the world possible and provide students with the time and forms to meet the world, meet themselves in relation to the world, and "work through" the complexities of such encounters' (Biesta, 2021, p. 17).

Mary's story also offers insights into inclusion and access (or lack of access/exclusion – which Mary was quite rightly frustrated about). In this regard, her 'story' offers an example of mud in relation to inclusive practice, whereby mud can be conceptualised as a medium for sensory integration; a sensory experience that is appealing from a range of perspectives. Mary chose and actively sought out this experience – she connected with the mud and the sticks – and the dogs. These are, therefore, artefacts for facilitating her enjoyment and engagement of a 'muddy moment'. Muddy play could, therefore, be channeled as a mechanism within support structures to build participation and inclusion for young people with Special Educational Needs and/or Disabilities (SEND). Like Mary, the young people in the second story sought out the sensory experience of sliding through mud on their stomachs and splashing through muddy puddles – which, had these been suggested as planned activities, would most likely have been dismissed by them as too childish.

The stories bring to mind an experience I had as an environmental youth worker. Two young women were helping construct a path to a bird hide, wiping their muddy hands on their faces, declaring it as good for their skin and an alternative to makeup. I recall their laughter as they watched each other playing with mud, smearing it on their skin, the poses they struck for the camera – 'jazz hands and muddy smiles' I captioned it in my head. The image lingers in my memories, becoming one of my 'magic moments' (Hayes & Prince, 2019). Reflecting on these muddy moments, I echo Powell's questions: have these moments been 'mediated by mud, induced by mud, inspired, provoked, suggested by mud?' (Powell in Somerville & Powell, 2019, p. 233) – the answer(s) depend(s) on your perspective(s). However, they were most definitely spontaneous, serendipitous – and muddy!

Skar et al. highlight that 'spontaneous play arises at events where there are fewer participants, in which children are able to stay in one place, when adults take a more relaxed and less intrusive approach, and where there are fewer formally organized (sic.) activities' (Skar et al., 2016b, p. 527). We cannot force these moments to happen; we cannot instruct young people (or adults) to play, have fun, or even guide them the same way as we may with younger children. Young people would perceive that as patronising and age-inappropriate. Instead, we need to create the necessary environment for young people to feel safe to be 'older children', to be childlike, and enjoy being together, outdoors, having fun. This can be achieved through thoughtful facilitation that includes modelling playful behaviour, being prepared to join in, perhaps as a play partner, or simply by standing back and allowing things to happen, enabling the nonhuman elements of the surroundings to suggest, invite, and make unplanned activities possible (Hackett & Rautio, 2019).

I believe there is a need for playful, creative approaches that allow people of all ages to have fun and feel comfortable being *with* nature rather than doing things to, in and for nature. The role of the teacher or facilitator is critical, and within this, effective communication – direct and indirect – is vital. This communication is more-than-human: it is entangled, embodied, and affective; it is temporal and spatial, forming a multi-modal way of answering the world. Within my research, I have argued that the need for playfulness and creativity extends beyond practice to research by utilising playful approaches to gathering and presenting data. What messages are we communicating if we say one thing but do another? By making the most of muddy moments, we also develop connections and valuable memories.

Concluding Thoughts

What is it about mud that is beneficial? Fruin makes a case for the 'open-endedness of mud as a play resource suited to supporting [young] children's critical thinking' (Fruin, 2020, p. 72). It is evocative and has sensory appeal – the smell, feel, sight of it, the noise it makes when we engage with it in its wet forms: squish, splatter, splash, splosh, slip, slop, plop, squelch – with mud, 'the world seems to be insistently present and demanding our response' (Somerville & Powell, 2018, p. 831). The world, through mud, demands attention. In its drier forms, we can let it run through our fingers, sifting it to remove debris and provide a nurturing space for seeds to sprout and plants to grow. We can pat it tenderly, bedding in plants we watch over as they transform and blossom, helping us look towards a future that may be distinctly different from our past. We may get frustrated at how it clings to our nails, skin, and hair and then reflect on the memories of how it got there as we vigorously scrub and wash it away. These external processes may provide a welcome relief from introspective processes, a reminder of life that exists outside of us, enabling us to develop a relationship with it – to feel a connection with others (human and nonhuman). When we share this experience, we have opportunities to develop new relationships, nurture existing relationships, and create memorable moments with psychological and emotional benefits that sustain us during more difficult times.

Reviewing literature for this chapter has highlighted the need for further research to explore young people's relationship with nature, embracing more contemporary posthuman approaches, which shift away from the dominant, anthropocentric approaches typically used to measure and increase young people's 'connection to nature'. The concept of 'answering the world', combined with embodied and material everyday practices that engage with popular culture, aligns with the participatory approaches youth and community workers use for research with young people (Cooper, 2017). Further research will help to understand the physical, psychological, and emotional benefits to adolescents of being outdoors and playing in/with mud. As this chapter illustrates, serendipitous encounters with mud foster creativity and spontaneity and promote overall well-being. To facilitate this, an environment must be created where young people can enjoy being together outdoors and having fun. We need to 'till the soil' for the seeds to grow.

As I reflected on the experiences shared in this chapter, I found myself dwelling on the muddy moments I have shared with others. They were silly, unexpected moments, yet I now realise how important they were in relational terms. As we laughed together, played together, or squished through mud, we connected in a way that enabled us to be together more meaningfully, to show care for each other and nature. They were moments where 'a relational sensitivity and a porousness to the world [was] enacted and felt' (Pettersen, 2024, p. 4), moments when 'chance encounters play[ed] vital roles in the unfolding of activities' (p. 12). I have relished revisiting these moments in a more mindful, dare I say, 'mudful' way, and I agree with Flanders and Swann (1957): mud certainly can be glorious. I encourage you to be responsive to serendipitous encounters with mud and make the most of muddy moments, to develop connections and valuable memories. Let's all look out for opportunities to 'wallow in glorious mud'.

CHAPTER 6

'No Badge Required': A Bucket School Approach to Support Teaching and Learning in the Outdoors

Louise Hawxwell[a] and Nicky Bolton[b]

[a]University of Edinburgh, UK
[b]Tattenhall Park Primary School, UK

ABSTRACT

Spending time in the outdoors has been recognised as having a positive impact on several aspects of children's lives. Educational settings and practitioners are recognised as being in an ideal position to provide outdoor learning (OL) opportunities and experiences. Despite the increase in attention towards using the outdoors for teaching and learning over recent years, concerns have been raised about practitioner knowledge of the outdoors. This has led to 'experts' rather than teachers providing OL experiences in schools. This potentially undermines teacher expertise and confidence, alongside limiting the opportunities offered by OL. This chapter presents a place-responsive, experiential, and hands-on approach to OL, known as 'Bucket School'. We demonstrate how all teachers can 'have a go' with Bucket School, helping them to approach OL with confidence, thereby removing 'imposter syndrome' for those involved in teaching and learning in the outdoors.

Introduction

The place where learning happens is an integral part of the learning experience and requires careful consideration to maximise opportunities offered to learners. Outdoor activities, where a 'rich combination of elements [are] embedded in local culture, history and environment', can be recognised as being both place and context-specific (Loynes, 2013, p. 140). School grounds and the local environment can be hugely significant to the lives of children in our classes (Beames et al., 2024) as not only their main space for playing and learning but also as a 'theatre of learning' (Bianchi & Feasey, 2011). Teachers, with their vast knowledge of curriculum and pedagogy, of their learners, schools, and local settings, are best placed for providing experiences in the outdoors.

The 'direct and deliberate' use of outdoor places can support 'innovative teaching-learning' (Khan et al., 2023, p. 385). In our chapter, we present *Bucket School*. A place-responsive, hands-on and practical approach to OL developed by Nicky Bolton (co-author of this chapter) whilst working as a science subject lead in primary school. This approach has been used with teachers and student teachers to help develop their confidence in taking learning outside, specifically for primary science lessons. We explain how *Bucket School* was developed, how it can be implemented to support learning both within and beyond curriculum structures, to meet curriculum intentions and other outcomes such as teamwork, enjoyment, and participation, with minimal resources – in fact often just a bucket!

Background Context

Following the definition of OL by Beames et al. (2024) offered in the introduction to this book, we too recognise OL as a hands-on, experiential, and practical pedagogical approach that includes learning in and about the world, and places around us, through and in a variety of ways and settings beyond the classroom, including school grounds, playgrounds, local spaces, and elsewhere. Over recent years, interest in OL has grown steadily, with the potential value of the outdoors and OL being widely documented both nationally and internationally through a wealth of research published highlighting the positive impacts and benefits. This includes improvements in health and wellbeing, increased academic achievement and progress, social and emotional development (see, e.g. DfES, 2006; Mannion et al., 2015; Natural England, 2016; and others).

Support for OL in Educational Policy

Following the publication of the *Education Outside the Classroom* report (Education and Skills Committee) in 2005, an increased emphasis was placed on OL nationally. This report noted several benefits of learning outdoors, including its potential for supporting academic achievement and attainment and development of social skills, especially for those children considered to be hard to reach. This report also highlighted patchy provision of OL in schools, and widespread concerns from teachers about time, funding, resources, and risk when offering outdoor opportunities. In response to this report, several initiatives were implemented, and further documents were published. The *Learning Outside the Classroom Manifesto* was published in 2006, setting out a shared vision and statements of intent for all those involved in providing outdoor opportunities for children and young people; this included individuals such as teachers, specific sites including schools and museums, along with organisations. The main aim of this manifesto is for 'every young person [to] experience the world beyond the classroom as an essential part of learning and personal development, whatever their age, ability or circumstances' (DfES, 2006, inside cover). In 2008, the 'LOtC Quality Badge' scheme was launched. This accreditation scheme enables those who provide OL opportunities to demonstrate both the quality of their provision alongside their commitment to health and safety and risk management. This scheme was designed to support teachers and schools in identifying suitable and appropriate settings and to relieve some of the concerns about risk raised by some teachers, as highlighted in the 2005 report. In 2009, increased government support for OL continued through the establishment of The Council for Learning Outside the Classroom (CLOtC) by the Department for Education and Skills (DfES). The CLOtC was given the responsibility for implementing and driving forward both the LOtC manifesto and the LOtC Quality Badge scheme. In 2008, Ofsted carried out an evaluation of OL provision across a range of education settings, including primary and secondary schools, highlighting how OL 'contributed significantly to raising standards and improving pupils' personal, social and emotional development' (Ofsted, 2008, p. 5). Published at a time when the government was actively promoting OL, *Learning Outside the Classroom: How far should you go?* shared examples of OL provision alongside how schools had been successful in overcoming several common barriers that had been highlighted in the *Education Outside the Classroom* report, thereby providing models for other schools and practitioners to consider and potentially implement.

In 2010, *Transforming Education Outside the Classroom* (House of Commons Children, Schools and Families Committee) was published. While this report was being written, a governmental priority for education in England was for primary schools to have more flexibility in their curriculum, enabling schools to offer a more broad, challenging, and engaging curriculum meeting the individual needs of their pupils. This flexibility would provide opportunities for schools and teachers to make use of the outdoors and OL experiences to best support their children. The Select Committee authoring this report queried why, (despite supposed increased autonomy in curriculum design for schools and teachers, the OL initiatives mentioned above, and the increase in research into OL), schools had not adopted OL 'more widely and more enthusiastically' (House of Commons Children, Schools and Families Committee, 2010, p. 9). Possible reasons suggested in the report included the lack of funding for OL, continued concerns from teachers over health and safety issues, and little attention to preparing future teachers for leading OL as part of initial teacher education. Recommendations from the committee to address these included increases in funding – to support the work of the CLOtC and to schools for trips and visits. Further proposals suggested making OL an entitlement in the National Curriculum, OL to be included as part of the inspection of schools, and for OL to be given a greater presence in initial teacher education programmes and teacher professional development.

Since the recommendations made in the 2010 *Transforming Education Outside the Classroom* report, there have been several changes in government along with differing priorities for education. With education being a devolved matter, there are considerable differences between the four nations of the United Kingdom in how these recommendations have been addressed and/or implemented into educational policy and practice. Based upon our own teaching experiences and contexts, we turn to England and Scotland.

England

At the time of writing OL is still neither an integral nor explicit part of educational policy or practice in England. Despite the development of new programmes of study across all subjects as part of the coalition government's focus on curriculum reform (DfE, 2010) taking place in the period *after* the recommendations for OL to be made an entitlement in the National Curriculum, there is little to no reference to OL as either a pedagogical approach or a specific discipline in the English National Curriculum. There is some implicit reference to the use of the outdoors in some subjects. For example, in Physical Education (PE), *outdoor adventurous activities* can be found within the programmes of study for Key Stages 2–4 (7–16 years of age). These outdoor-based activities are intended to support the development of skills such as teamwork and problem-solving. Another implicit mention of the outdoors can be found in Key Stage 1 science (5–7 years of age), where an aim for the subject is for children to gain experience in 'looking more closely at the natural and humanly constructed world around them' (DfE, 2013). Regarding school inspections, the provision of OL is not included in the school inspection framework handbook as either an indicator of educational quality or as part of an ambitious, sequenced, rigorous, and broad curriculum (Ofsted, 2024). OL is not referred to in either the *Initial Teacher Training Core Content Framework* (DfE, 2024a, 2024b) or the *Teachers' Standards* (DfE, 2021). Within the later document, the statement of being able to 'plan other out-of-class activities to consolidate and extend the knowledge and understanding pupils have acquired' within *Standard 4: Plan and teach well-structured lessons* implies the use of places other than the classroom (DfE, 2021, p. 11) but the outdoors is not explicitly mentioned.

Scotland

In Scotland, strategic developments within education policy have enabled OL to be explicitly and successfully integrated into practice. OL is clearly positioned as an entitlement for all learners and an expectation of all teachers (Education Scotland, 2011), through several initiatives that have been implemented into practice. This includes OL being fully embedded into the Curriculum for Excellence framework (Scottish Government, 2004) as an approach for teaching and learning across all curriculum subject areas, with guidance and support being provided for teachers through publications such as *Curriculum for Excellence through Outdoor Learning* (Learning & Teaching Scotland, 2010) and *Outdoor Learning: Practical guidance, ideas and support for teachers and practitioners in Scotland* (Education Scotland, 2011). OL is also one of the major strands of the *Learning for Sustainability* agenda (Scottish Government, 2012; revised in 2023) and is clearly outlined in the professional standards for students, probationers and qualified teachers (GTCS, 2021). The recent national discussion on education *All Learners in Scotland Matter* (2023) also highlighted the importance of OL activities throughout a young person's education. This unified support from educational and political sectors within Scotland through initiatives, such as those described, has been recognised as 'facilitating the process of moving from the rhetoric and policies to enabling the transformation required within schools' (Christie et al., 2016, p. 114), enabling OL to be embraced and embedded into teaching and learning practices by the education profession without the requirements for additional qualifications or training.

Barriers to OL

Barriers to OL have been identified impacting on both provision and access to the outdoors (see, e.g. Barrable et al., 2022;

Barrable & Lakin, 2020; Hawxwell, 2019; Natural England, 2016). Research has highlighted how consumerism and commodification of the outdoors has resulted in tensions and dilemmas for practice, as well as for stakeholders, which in turn could be a potential barrier to outdoor access and OL provision (Kemp, 2019). The development of Forest School across the United Kingdom is an example of a 'corporate turn' in OL (Leather, 2018, p. 5). Forest School was initially developed from the concept of *frilutsliv*, the open-air culture that is an important aspect of everyday life and education in Scandinavia. The term *Forest School* was conceived by a group of early years lecturers from Bridgewater College, Somerset, England, who set up a forest school in their college creche following a visit to Denmark in 1993 to observe early years practices. Their forest school included many of the outdoor activities observed in Denmark, such as using natural materials and resources in play, free exploration of the environment around the creche including climbing trees. The process of transferring activities from one context to another has the potential to generate new experiences as in the case of the forest school set up in the college. But this transference can also create the possibility of *McDonaldizing* [sic.] the experience into a 'replicable structure, often with the same elements everywhere', reducing it down to 'a small number of key elements that can be branded and marketed globally' (Loynes, 2013, p. 141) as in the case of 'Forest School' in the UK, where there is an agreed definition and six defining principles for all Forest School practices. Forest School is not a term used in Scandinavia, nor do they have forest schools. They have '*skovbørnehaver*' – forest kindergartens, '*skovegrupper*' – forest or woodland groups, and '*naturbørnehaver*' – nature kindergartens, alongside other early years settings that make use of the outdoors (Williams-Siegfredsen, 2012).

For some teachers, their own previous experiences of OL may be mainly based on those offered during school residentials. These activities are usually delivered by qualified instructors at outdoor adventure or activity centres, owned by external organisations and companies. These organisations and individuals will have recognised accreditation, such as the CLOtC's Quality Mark (discussed previously), National Outdoor Learning

Award (NOLA) issued by the Institute for Outdoor Learning (IOL), or specific qualifications such as Forest School Leader or those gained during outdoor instructor trainings. Awards and qualifications such as these position the organisations and individuals as having the accepted professional capital, or 'badge' for teaching outdoors (Leather, 2018). This 'creep of "experts"' (Cosgriff, 2017, p. 24) could potentially further undermine the agency and confidence of teachers to provide OL experiences for their classes. It could also potentially limit opportunities for learning in the outdoors as outdoor experiences may be reduced to rigid and set timetabled sessions or to one-off encounters, depending on the availability of these 'experts' (Kemp, 2019; Leather, 2018).

A further barrier identified is linked to the performativity agenda within many education systems driven by league tables, testing regimes, external pressures, such as inspections, and other curriculum demands. In many schools, particularly in England, 'inspections drive provision' (Prince & Diggory, 2023, p. 3). As noted earlier, there is no reference to OL in the inspection handbook for schools (Ofsted, 2024), therefore, Senior Leadership Teams will require assurance that any OL provision not only addresses the requirements of the curriculum but also contributes favourably and positively to any feedback and reports from inspectors. This may position OL as a possible educational risk (Kemp & Pagden, 2018) and create additional pressures and demands on teachers.

Teacher confidence is a major factor linked to OL provision. This may be due to concerns about health and safety (Hawxwell, 2019; Ross et al., 2007), which was identified as an important area to address back in 2005, including worries about behaviour of the children when outdoors (Hawxwell, 2019), or feeling they do not have the knowledge or understanding of the outdoors to be able to teach confidently. This may include identification of different living things, including trees and other species, and/or what can be done with the children while outside. Several authors, including Richard Louv (2010), Robert Macfarlane (2017), and George Monbiot (2016), describe a generation of children who are growing up in an indoor world, lacking basic vocabulary of nature, who are obsessed with digital, and disconnected from the outdoors. Louv (2010) refers to this lack of contact with the natural world as *nature-deficit disorder*. It is important to acknowledge that many younger teachers may have grown up in this *nature-deficit* culture as part of the *disconnected generation* and so may require further support and encouragement to take learning outdoors.

Childhood experiences in the outdoors have also been identified as being significant in decision-making by teachers to take learning outdoors (see, e.g. Ernst, 2013). Those with positive experiences may wish to replicate these with their classes, but it is possible that some teachers may not have such positive experiences, subsequently having mixed or negative feelings about the outdoors. This may mean some might feel uncomfortable or uneasy while outside. It is important to acknowledge and be aware of this.

Introducing Bucket School

Findings such as those discussed set the challenge of helping every teacher – whether they are experienced, newly qualified or student – to view the outdoors as a place for learning and teaching that does not require specialist training or qualifications; a place where quality-first teaching can take place effectively and teachers feel confident to deliver learning experiences across the curriculum.

To support teacher confidence and to embed more frequent practice of OL in the school she was working in at the time, Nicky Bolton developed *Bucket School*. This versatile and portable model for OL can be tailored to satisfy many curriculum objectives, address barriers to OL outlined above, and has a multitude of outcomes. It allows for creative, and messy, learning, whilst also providing a way to promote a love of learning outdoors. Using Bucket School allows teachers and children the opportunity to find a myriad of investigative learning opportunities in and around the school environment. The vignette below, written by Nicky, outlines the way in which this approach to OL evolved within a mainstream primary school setting.

The model of 'Bucket School' evolved several years ago when I was asked to develop an outdoor area at school to encourage the teachers to take teaching and learning outdoors. Educational research at the time advocated that this approach to learning could potentially increase pupil progress by an average of nine months extra schooling (DfES, 2006). After fundraising and consulting with colleagues, we designed and built a large wooden outdoor classroom pergola structure with seating areas, moveable workbenches, blackout blinds so that it could be used as a dark area, and a blackboard. It seemed the perfect structure to tempt teachers to take their learning outdoors.

For the first few weeks of a beautifully warm summer term, there was a flurry of excited use. Teachers used the outdoor classroom for science lessons, reading sessions, the playing of musical instruments, and even dissected owl pellets! But as we approached autumn, the leaves began to gather under the seating, the spiders took up residence, and play equipment began to be stored inside on rainy days. The outdoor classroom weathered the winter, but by the following summer, it had lost its smell of freshly shaved wood and was damp and dusty, full of insects, scooters and outdoor plastic building blocks. The building of the outdoor pergola had, sadly, not enticed teachers to take the bold step of taking learning outdoors.

Desperate to revive its use, the eco-council held a family day and swept out the classroom, washed down the wood and scrubbed the decking. For a few weeks, teachers used the space again, but interest waned as the weather became colder. Interested to find out why this structure had not captured the teachers' imaginations, we held a staff meeting to discuss how we could use the outdoor pergola more effectively. Teachers could identify opportunities in the curriculum to use the outdoor space, however they had a multitude of worries about taking learning outdoors. Time constraints were a noteworthy factor. With the demands of the National Curriculum, teachers felt they could not afford the luxury of spending time out of the classroom and felt the content of their outdoor lessons may not comprehensively meet curriculum requirements. Behaviour was also a concern. Teachers were worried that pupils would not maintain focus outside and that OL brought multiple health and safety risks, potentially needing risk assessments, which would take considerable time to write. Most significantly, teachers felt they were not 'trained' to take learning outdoors, suggesting that we develop a 'Forest School' to promote OL. Interestingly, several teachers felt that having one fixed classroom structure restricted study to only one area of the school grounds rather than over a wider space. Evidently, a different approach was needed to encourage them to venture outdoors with their classes.

The challenge was to enable every teacher to view the outdoors as a place for effective, flexible learning that did not require specialist training, such as the awards and qualifications mentioned previously. And so, Bucket School began!

How Bucket School Can Be Implemented into Your Practice

The vision for Bucket School is simple. The principle behind the Bucket School model is to allow every teacher to explore their curriculum/s creatively and practically through a hands-on and place-responsive approach and to help develop teacher confidence in taking learning outdoors.

At its simplest level, buckets can be used as something to sit on in a teaching circle, providing an instant, outdoor classroom (see Fig. 6.1). The buckets give children a clear signpost that learning outdoors is about to take place. Buckets can also be something to collect with, something to label, or even something to launch rockets from! As buckets are easily moved to different locations and spaces, in Bucket School children and

Fig. 6.1. Bucket School in Action
The Buckets create an instant space for teaching and learning, including seating. The circle also creates a collective space and sense of togetherness for the class.

Source: Photo: Nicky Bolton/Louise Hawxwell.

teachers have the freedom to move their classroom around the school grounds, going beyond this space when required. It is flexible and organic, with the possibilities only being limited by the teacher's imagination and creativity. It is cheap, with the only initial cost being a class set of buckets, so a fraction of the cost of building an outdoor classroom.

Bucket School creates opportunities for children and their teachers to explore ideas in a hands-on and exploratory way, using both natural and manmade resources. Bucket School, as an outdoor teaching and learning approach, has the potential to make subjects 'vivid and interesting' (Ofsted, 2008, p. 7), providing 'relevance and depth to the curriculum' (Learning and Teaching Scotland, 2010, p. 5). This, in turn, has a positive influence on children's behaviour. In contrast with many teachers' expectations, behaviour outdoors in a structured Bucket School is often superior to that within the four walls of the classroom.

When implementing this approach in a school, it is important for staff to appreciate *how* Bucket School can be used across the curriculum to take their learning outdoors. Every teacher will have their own perception and ideas of how to use Bucket School. A crucial first step is to scrutinise the long-term curriculum plans, creatively, as a staff team and to identify opportunities, across the academic year, when Bucket School can be used to enhance learning. It may be that teachers plan a very short session using Bucket School simply as a vehicle for collecting objects for a science lesson or as a seat to use whilst sketching outdoors – the key is to keep sessions short, simple, and frequent in the formative sessions of Bucket School, to allow staff to realise what an effective tool Bucket School can be.

If a Bucket School session goes well and satisfies clear curriculum outcomes, this may also mitigate some of the trepidation felt by some teachers due to their previous negative experiences in the outdoors and will encourage teachers to take the bold step of taking their OL further afield. Delivering Bucket School in the school grounds in the early stages of using this pedagogy can support teachers in developing their knowledge of and skills of managing risks within the relative safety of their school environment, with the reassurance that other staff are nearby. Positive experiences delivering outdoor sessions in a 'safe' onsite, outdoor setting are crucial in supporting the development of self-efficacy for teaching outdoors, which can increase both confidence and motivation to take learning outdoors (Barrable et al., 2022). The flexibility of the Bucket School approach provides opportunities for teachers to be in a myriad of different spaces and places.

Teachers must acknowledge that whilst outdoors, children will encounter plants, animals, and other outdoor phenomena that they may not be able to name or explain. Teachers should not feel they have to be 'experts' about the flora and fauna of the outdoors – this should not be a barrier to taking learning outdoors. Continuing conversations and researching the unknown, as a teacher/pupil partnership back in the classroom, is a strong teaching tool and one which demonstrates to a child that everyone is always learning.

Three Quick Bucket School Takeaways

It should be remembered Bucket School is not a prescriptive pedagogy. The whole concept of this approach is that when children hear they are doing Bucket School, they know they are taking their learning outdoors – it is a simple as that! The only limit to Bucket School is your imagination. However, here are a few tried and tested Bucket School favourites.

Food Webbing

This can be conducted in two ways. The first involves sticking pictures of different animals and plants from a known ecosystem on the front of each bucket. Using a printed food web of the ecosystem as a reference point, children sit in a circle on their

Fig. 6.2. **Different Learning and Teaching Activities Can Be Carried Out in Bucket School in all Weathers.**
Source: **Photo: Nicky Bolton.**

buckets and draw chalk lines between their buckets to demonstrate connections between the different organisms in the ecosystem (see Fig. 6.2. top image). These connections can also be made using string. Sticking a plastic pocket to the front of each bucket will allow teachers to interchange different pictures and resource sheets, allowing the bucket to be used for activities across the curriculum.

When Bucket School was initially developed, the focus was on primary science, so many of the first activities created linked to aspects of the science curriculum, including helping children in developing knowledge and understanding of concepts along with the development of scientific enquiry skills. However, Bucket School can be used in so many ways – for collecting natural materials to make stone age paints, sorting and classifying activities linked to found objects in the outdoors, creating 3D DT structures using natural materials found in the outdoors. Bucket School can be used across the whole curriculum. It has limitless curriculum opportunities and the possibilities for Bucket School sessions are endless.

3D Maths Games

Using a sheet showing the mathematical language of different properties of shapes, two children sit back to back. The first child has a bundle of sticks. As the second child describes the properties of a chosen shape, one property at a time, the first child creates the shape in front of them (see Fig. 6.2. image 2, carried out with sticks *and* snow!). This is a very effective way to practise mathematical vocabulary and can be extended to 3D shapes if teachers and children are feeling ambitious.

Making a Skeleton

Creating skeletons with sticks collected in buckets is a great assessment tool. At the beginning of a series of lessons learning about the structure of a skeleton, children can be asked to create a skeleton after gathering sticks in their buckets. Children can add labels on whiteboards to indicate their prior knowledge of different bones or functions of the skeleton. After a series of lessons in the classroom, the children then repeat the activity to demonstrate the knowledge they have gained. This can also be extended to creating skeletons of animals.

Bucket School Goes International

The concept of Bucket school is entirely transportable across different contexts and settings. Several years ago, Nicky visited Uganda to support a schools twinning project. Many of the schools visited had very limited space in the classrooms, and this restricted the way in which a 'hands-on' curriculum could be delivered. Modelling Bucket School to the teachers in these schools allowed them to generate ideas across their own curricula so that they could take their learning outdoors into other spaces around the school (see Fig. 6.3). As many school budgets in Uganda were very limited, we discovered that some of the buckets used to transport cooking oils could be used instead, thereby providing a free resource to support the development of this initiative. A particularly memorable session involved a Bucket School drumming session. This session clearly showed the versatility of this teaching model across the curriculum. Brainstorming ideas for Bucket School sessions with these staff showed just how open ended the Bucket School model can be.

Fig. 6.3. Bucket School in Uganda.

Conclusion

An aim of the LOtC Manifesto is for 'every young person [to] experience the world beyond their classroom' (LOtC Manifesto, DfES, 2006). We believe that Bucket School not only meets this aim but goes much further. We believe Bucket School can:

- improve teacher confidence in taking learning outside the classroom;
- provide opportunities to explore concepts from all elements of national curricula practically in an outdoor context;
- inspire curiosity about the natural environment;
- increase self-esteem and self-confidence;
- improve social skills;
- improve motivation and encourage concentration;
- contribute to children's knowledge and understanding;
- allow teachers at all levels to gain new perspectives on seeing children responding in a more child-led environment;
- create ripple effects beyond Bucket School – children (and students) will take their experiences home and tell family and friends.

Mark Leather (2018) notes that practitioners who are skilled are competent risk managers, understand the importance of play, have a knowledge of pedagogical activities, and hold a teaching qualification; then further qualifications to teach outdoors are not required. Beames et al. (2024) agree, stating 'almost all learning outdoors does not require specialist equipment and expert instructors' (p. x). We wholeheartedly agree! We believe taking learning outdoors does not require extra qualifications or training or a badge. As we have shown, Bucket School does not require additional or costly qualifications, and it does not require a badge, or specialist equipment. All that is needed is imagination, enthusiasm, the outdoors, and a bucket!

PART 3

Continuing the Journey of Place-responsive Pedagogy in Outdoor Learning

CHAPTER 7

The Next Generation of Learning Outside: Fostering Place-responsive Pedagogy in Initial Teacher Education

Lucy Sors, Jen Huntsley and Stephanie Jach

York St John University, UK

ABSTRACT

This chapter explores how practice embedded in an outdoor learning (OL) module in initial teacher education (ITE) has evolved in response to place, people, time and context. We exemplify the impact of experiential learning on student participation, engagement and ownership of their education. Drawing on student voice alongside practitioner inquiry, the chapter proposes how teacher development for OL can be supported by Korthagen's model of realistic teacher education (2017). We make the case for place-responsive pedagogy in teacher training that supports authentic and connected teaching and learning. Student-teachers experience this on different levels as 'person-learner-teacher', developing their educational philosophy and professional teaching repertoire. We demonstrate how brave steps in ITE can take learning beyond four walls and develop context-responsive, creative pedagogical approaches to enhance student–teacher understanding, experience and critical engagement (Waite, 2017).

Chapter dedicated in memorandum to a great student of outdoor learning, Conor Pearce John Fallon (1991–2024).

Introduction

This book has offered theoretical stances, research and empirical examples of place-responsive pedagogy in different OL contexts. In this chapter, we expand the conversation to undergraduate university students undertaking a 3-year degree in Primary Education with Qualified Teacher Status (QTS). We explore the responsive enactment of theory and practice within a module on OL. This module brings together place-responsive pedagogy, experiential learning, slow pedagogy and world-centred theories of learning. From this theoretical base, we explore the development of student–teachers' professional and personal skills through their experiences as *learners*, their formation as *teachers* and their *personal* connections. Our case study will outline how collaborative approaches between academic staff and student–teachers can inform learning design, and how authentic, experiential learning can be effectively interwoven with higher education (HE) study. Our analysis draws upon 'realistic teacher education' (Korthagen et al., 2001) and is informed by a place-responsive framework, staff and student–teacher perspectives. As *facilitators*[1] of the OL module, we engage in practitioner enquiry to explore how the module has evolved through interaction and response. Student–teacher views of experiences on the module demonstrate how OL can enlighten personal teaching philosophies to influence teaching and learning in primary schools.

OL in Initial Teacher Education

The OL module is part of a suite of final year 'elective' modules developed by a team in ITE at York St John University. Student–teachers on the precipice of their careers choose from an area of specialism as part of a broader vision for primary education. The final assessment across all electives takes the form of a creative artefact. This requires student–teachers to persuade a professional audience of the benefits of their specialist area

---

[1] A co-constructive approach has challenged our view of the job-title – *lecturer* – and the power dynamics it encompasses; we feel the term *facilitator* is more accurate in this OL context.

through a format of their choice. The assessment design rests on the understanding of the need for 'a robust creative agency, that allows [student-teachers] to resist performative pressures, developing ways of teaching that have meaning for them' (Raymond, 2019, IV). This approach also aligns with the Inclusive Education Framework, which advocates for 'assessments embedded in "real world" scenarios' linked to wider context and future careers (Hull University, 2023). 'Authentic creativity' (Raymond, 2019) is, therefore, a key driver for practice on the OL module, which provides a range of opportunities for student–teachers to pragmatically explore their skills in meaningful ways and establish ownership of their learning. Genuine, connected experience is central to the module's design and delivery as part of an ongoing process of review, response and redesign based on experiences and feedback from student-teachers.

The OL module centres around experiential opportunities that explore a range of related theories. It aims to provide students with first-hand, situated experiences to gain insight from the perspectives of the learners they will be working with as teachers. Place-responsive practice supports student–teachers to develop skills, knowledge and confidence to use OL. Put most succinctly by one student–teacher, reflecting on their experiences in a Forest School workshop: 'How can we teach children how to climb trees if we haven't experienced it ourselves?' Student-teachers' critical thinking is developed by facilitators' questioning, for example:

- *How would you use this with your class?*
- *What benefits/limitations/considerations do you foresee in this approach?*
- *How does this choice of outdoor pedagogy enhance children's experiences of learning?*

This is consolidated through reflection, research and exploration of theory around each experience. Place-responsive pedagogy positions the outdoors as a starting point to facilitate metacognition and *transversal skills* development: enquiry and creativity; interpersonal and intrapersonal skills; critical thinking and global citizenship (UNESCO, 2016). 'Learning through places' offer student-teachers 'holistic, cross-curricular ways of learning outdoors' (Beames et al., 2024, p.59). For example, scientific enquiry focussing on sustainability is realised through art, design, technology and drama as they explore different methods of seed dispersal in the university's wildflower meadow. As in other experiences, student–teachers *choose* their responses to workshop stimuli; some make paper model seeds to illustrate flight dispersal, whereas others may role-play as animals, transporting real or imaginary seeds across the space in various ways. Open pedagogical approaches have led to a range of responses as student–teachers explore theories, perspectives and worldviews (Beames et al., 2024, p. 17). Time is presented as a key element of this, pushing student–teachers beyond the comfort zones of university regimented timetables, instead 'experiencing learning under the open sky' (Kelly, 2022, p. 187). Slow pedagogical approaches on the module foster incidental learning and nature/place/people/self-connection opportunities, realised perhaps as student-teachers gently rock in hammocks and whittle writing tools around a softly burning fire in the woods.

Student–teachers participate differently (conceptually and experientially), encountering 'a highly personal but social and ecological meaning-making and learning journey that slowly unfolds' (Payne & Wattchow, 2009, p. 28). Ownership of learning is evident in the array of interpretations of campus; some through the creation of 'pigeon-eye view messy-maps', others through Tik-Toks of 'the journey of a snail' in a micro-exploration of small spaces in familiar places. Further afield, student–teachers engage in the stimulus of a 'Roman Tour of York' to plan and deliver a *microteach*; an 'approximation of practice' (Grossman et al., 2009), to rehearse teaching skills in a low-stakes environment with their peers. Applying a range of pedagogical approaches in their city has led to joyful, playful encounters (Woods, 2017): a dramatic re-enactment of marching Roman soldiers in tortoise formation; a peaceful creation of a mosaic made from natural materials near York's Roman ruins. Other experiences introduce student-teachers to OL and nature-connection, such as exploring the university allotment; designing outdoor spaces; 'storying the outdoors' river walks to uncover the secrets of fairies; and an introduction to Forest School activities in a local woodland. Structured reflection is facilitated by open dialogue and the use of a shared virtual space as a reflective journal (Padlet). Ongoing critical conversations around theory and practice (sharing their own and others' reflections) support in understanding *why* OL is important in primary education and *how* pupils will encounter this on different levels, as student–teachers have experienced themselves.

Integrating Theory and Practice

Throughout the planning and delivery of the module, we have increasingly engaged with systematic inquiry into our own practice and student–teachers' learning. This started with a shared philosophical understanding of OL as a 'good thing', based on our experiences and commitment to transform practice as we had done as teachers. Our starting point for the module was our own practices as primary teachers and our personal lives; our OL '*habitus*' which we interrogated on different levels (see Akram, 2023, illustrated in Fig. 1.2 in this book). Our shared reflections and journey of *practitioner inquiry* led us to consider a theoretical framework based on a model of realistic teacher education

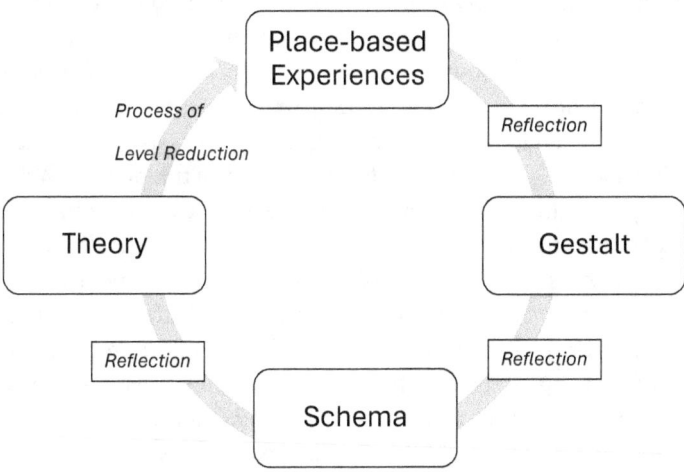

Fig. 7.1. Re-conceptualised Model of Korthagen and Lagerwerf's *Three Levels of Changing Teacher Behaviour.*
Source: Adapted from Korthagen & Lagerwerf. (2001, p. 191).

(Korthagen et al., 2001). We present a reconceptualisation of this model in Fig. 7.1 to demonstrate to the reader how and why we teach the module the way we do.

Gestalts are 'an internal, unconscious conglomerate' of 'images, feelings, notions, values, needs or behavioral [*sic*] inclinations' that are triggered by our experiences with the external world (Korthagen, 2017, p. 533). Clear links between Korthagen's 'gestalt' and Bourdieu's notion of '*habitus*' (1977) relate to the embodiment of cultural capital in response to environment and social structures which have contributed to shaping a sense of self. This relates to personal, professional and socio-cultural knowledge informed by concrete experiences. Continuous, automatic, routine teacher disposition (*habitus*) is guided by *gestalts*, rather than theory, or even conscious, rational thought (Korthagen, 2017). While gestalts tend to be unconscious, through reflection the teacher may start to understand connections between gestalts: the beginning of *schematisation*.

A *schema* is 'a conscious mental map, easily accessible for introspection' to understand the 'network of relationships between concepts and notions' (Korthagen, 2017, p. 535). Korthagen suggests that two cognitive processes characterise the transition from *gestalts* to *schemata*. First, the teacher becomes conscious of *gestalts* through reflection. Second, they engage in a process of '*desituating* the knowledge derived from various specific situations' (Korthagen, 2017, p. 535, *original emphasis*). Initially, knowledge gained through teaching experience is likely to be situation-specific: what is needed for this activity in this place with this group of children at this time. Subsequently, we evaluate learning experiences through reflection on intended and unintended learning outcomes (Beames et al., 2024). Knowledge becomes less situation-specific, more generalised and transferable to a new setting. Teachers draw on this and adapt practice to support progressively complex reciprocal interactions between people – place – context (activity) which take place over time (*proximal processes* – Bronfenbrenner & Morris, 1998, see Chapter 3 in this book). Experience, practice and reflection support teachers to assimilate and accommodate new understanding within a schema of OL.

Korthagen (2017) suggests that practicing teachers operate predominantly at the gestalt and schema level, due to pre-occupations with knowing 'how to act in specific situations' (p. 535). The gradual process of becoming more conscious and analytical of connections between these extensive mental maps, along with a logical ordering of schemata content, can be described as theory formation: *why we choose to do what we do*. In practice, teachers are likely to draw on gestalt and schema knowledge rather than academic theory. However, theory that is well understood and meaningful is more likely to influence schema knowledge and require less conscious thought. The translation of theory to schema, and schema to gestalt, is described as *level reduction*. Behaviours become increasingly automatic, so concentration is directed to other aspects of teaching. Through level reduction, we understand that we work with a 'practical knowledge' drawn from 'research-based theoretical frameworks' (Korthagen, 2017, p. 536). Having explained the underpinning theoretical model of our practice, we now explore how we designed the OL module.

Designing a Place-responsive Module

In our first planning meeting we started with the question: *'What is outdoor learning and why is it important to primary education?'* This led to an instinctive undertaking of narrative inquiry through a conversation centred around 'a multi-dimensional exploration of experience involving temporality (past, present, future), interaction (personal and social), and location (place)' (Clandinin & Connelly, 2004, p. 576). Stories of our personal and professional journeys in OL weaved a rich tapestry of shared perspectives. We shared disappointment around restrictions in making use of the outdoors due to constraints of curriculum demands and other challenges to OL. We celebrated successes where we had taken learning outside with a range of children from diverse backgrounds, overcoming structural and socio-cultural barriers. We noted each others' skills and confidence in 'reflection-in-action' moments when we had negotiated the demands of conflicted, complex, unpredictable problems in OL through 'professional artistry' (Schön, 1987). Such artistry involves a deep practical knowledge of OL which emerges from well-developed schemata and theory-level understanding

(Korthagen et al., 2001). Conversations circled back to enduring issues of social injustice, loss of access to the outdoors and barriers to nature connection (e.g. see Waite 2020). We thus recognised the challenge of working with student–teachers, who would have varying experience of, with and in the outdoors. We concluded that repeated and frequent outdoor encounters had to be high on the agenda in order to provide embodied sensory-perceptual experiences alongside conceptual-theoretical development (Payne & Wattchow, 2009). We agreed on a 'coherent meshing of indoor and outdoor sites for learning' (Beames et al., 2017, p. 82) to support student-centred practice, ownership and participation.

Responsiveness guides our practice on the OL module. In each session, we bring personal responses (as parents, outdoor enthusiasts, researchers), and professional responses (as teachers and teacher–educators) facilitating emerging connections and answering student–teachers' needs and interests. Above all, we respond to opportunities (practical, experiential and theoretical) offered by places and sites of learning planned (or unplanned) on the module. Place-responsive pedagogy presented itself to us as a theoretical driver for teaching and learning. Different experiences and interactions between places and facilitators lead us to 'reccy' possibilities. Place-responsiveness develops as a creative process, as we explore exciting new teaching and learning contexts (Wattchow, 2021). The site of experience is thus prioritised as a 'framework within which students can construct their own learning' (Lieberman & Hoody, 1998 in Sobel, 2013, p. 15). Student–teachers' experiences are inextricably linked to the places we choose to situate workshops.

Situational and relational activities foster interactions on different planes of responsiveness. Student–teachers are frequently asked to reflect upon their deepening personal knowledge of OL in relation to their teaching philosophy. This develops through a range of place-responsive encounters. They realise the importance of interacting with place as they develop increasing enthusiasm for OL. This is a critical endeavour, whereby student-teachers are encouraged to consider past and present conflicts, differences and power relations inherent in the places we encounter – and beyond (Beames et al, 2024; Greunewald, 2003). Their *habitus* develops critical thinking, theory, practice and experience across different planes. A central value they repeatedly encounter is the transformative potential of OL in relation to social justice: its ability to 'speak truth to power' (Beames et al., 2024, p. 20). Students explore conflicts around access to the outdoors and engage with issues of inclusion, exclusion, disadvantage and privilege. They realise that values, knowledge and understanding have a significant influence on pupils' connections and relationships to the natural world (Barrable & Lakin, 2020). As facilitators, we respond to student–teachers' developing personal knowledge by provoking further reflection. We encourage them to step outside of their comfort zones to explore the potential of OL and of themselves in relation to understanding teaching and learning as 'place-essential' (Mannion et al., 2011, in Beames et al., 2024, p. 60). Student–teachers' contributions to our shared 'Padlet' demonstrate their personal journeys as well as their learning journey throughout the module.

Experiential learning provides exciting opportunities for co-construction, with student–teachers taking increased responsibility for their learning as they connect with OL. This entails a dialogic and reciprocal exchange, gradually moving learning beyond familiar, immediate, intimate spaces, to places that could be distant and strange (Sobel, 2013). Facilitators address barriers for student–teachers who might be initially hesitant due to a reliance on safer-feeling sedentary learning experiences. They gain confidence and develop ownership, consciously moving beyond the mindset of typical structures of academic learning. The module pushes 'pedagogical possibilities of (re)imagining and practicing a sense of space in experiential learning', challenging familiar indoor teaching to explore 'wilder realms of discovery' (Payne & Wattchow, 2009, p. 24).

Student–teachers' responses inspire us to teach outdoors as much as possible. As facilitators, we share and reflect on our teaching as a constant cycle: 'How did we respond to that place?', leading to 'how did student-teachers connect to the place/theory/pedagogy?'. 'What ifs...' (Biesta, 2017) compel our practice forward. Through ongoing narrative enquiry, we build 'desituated knowledge' (Korthagen, 2017, p. 535) and become increasingly conscious of OL gestalts informed by childhood, parenthood, teaching experiences and the current global context. Through dialogic reflection, our schemata become more detailed as we analyse conceptual connections. This allows us to develop a critical and reflexive approach informed by student voice and perspectives, which leads to a continuous process of deconstruction and reconstruction, and an ongoing 'conversation' between experiential learning and academic learning (Payne & Wattchow, 2009, p. 28).

The module facilitates transformation of *habitus* of student–teachers in a way that better prepares them for realistic practice, to act as agents of change and to enable access to OL for all children. The model of realistic teacher education guides our practice as facilitators, creating learning experiences that allow gestalts to form and prompting reflection that supports the development of schemata. Through reflection and level reduction, student–teachers assimilate and accommodate knowledge, dispositions and attitudes based on theory that is meaningful to them. It is not just that they understand theory and pedagogies (e.g. slow pedagogy, place-responsive education, experiential learning, etc.), it is also that they *know how to enact them* in practice.

Developing OL as a Person-Learner-Teacher

A framework of *person–learner–teacher* emerged in response to a fellow academic's observation of two OL workshops, who noted a responsive process situated around the significance of place.

> *Lucy, Jen and Stephanie are always communicating with students on several levels simultaneously: as* **learners**, *as emerging* **teachers**, *and as sensing, feeling* **human beings**. *In the community garden and on the fairy trail, conversations were nurtured around students' emotional* **responses** *and family memories of food growing or the natural world, as much as about teaching strategies or lesson plans.*
>
> Blog extract, Heinemeyer, 2022 (our emphasis)

Around the three nodes of *person–learner–teacher* identified by Heinemeyer, we analyse practice, reflections and student voice to identify examples of *theory-to-schema* translation. We suggest this supports student–teachers to deepen the complexity of their OL schemata, thus strengthening connection between theory and practice. We demonstrate this theory-level understanding using a mind map, as suggested by Korthagen (2017, p. 536). This shows the connections between different schemata and informs an analysis of student–teacher interviews. We aim to illustrate how responsive approaches facilitate reflection on gestalts and level reduction of theory. Distilling a complex theory-level mind-map in response to student voice (expanded below) revealed that student–teachers also experienced their learning on these three different levels by interactively responding in different places. This is presented in Fig. 7.2.

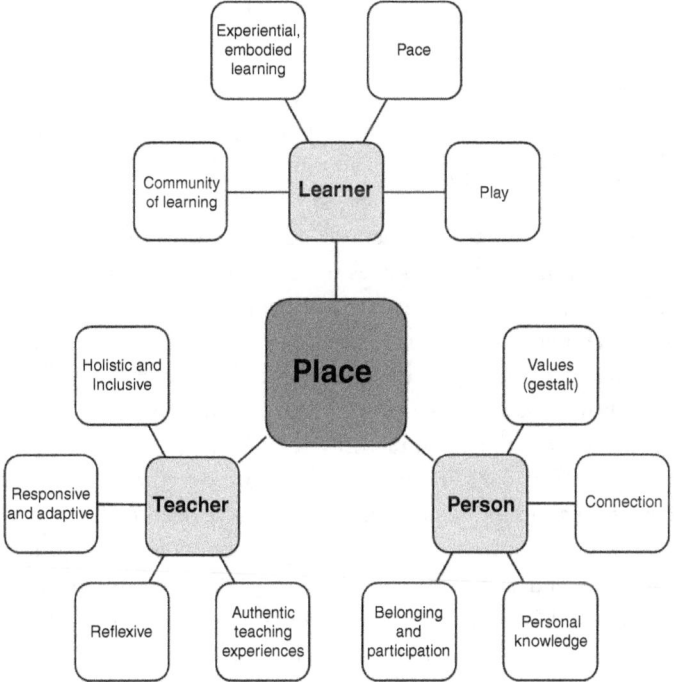

Fig. 7.2. 'Level Reduction' Mindmap of the OL Module.

In our analysis of narrative interviews completed by six student–teachers post-module (pseudonymously known as Lily, Lara, Rachel, Amber, Emily and Eve), we noted emergent themes and examples which linked to each of the three lenses *person, learner* and *teacher*. The student-teachers' responses suggested they had developed 'practical knowledge that is based on research-based theoretical frameworks' (Korthagen, 2017, p. 536), indicating that, through reflection, their understanding of OL had moved beyond that of gestalt to schema and, in some cases, theory.

Place

At the centre of the mind map is '*place*', reflecting the principles of authentic, connected and situated learning underpinning all practice on the module. Interactions are illustrated by connecting lines in Fig. 7.2. Ideas explored throughout this book support the central positioning of place. We now expand on *person–learner–teacher* as they have developed through place-responsive interactions within student–teachers' encounters.

Person

As a *person*, student–teachers experience the outdoors on a corporal level (Payne & Wattchow, 2009) and notice their thoughts, feelings, and **values** about OL (*gestalt*). Connecting to experience supported them to develop 'ways of meeting the world and meeting themselves in relation to the world' (Biesta, 2021, p. 16). Student–teachers are encouraged to *feel* nature connectedness, to encounter the outdoors as being *with* nature and places rather than being *in* nature and places (Payne & Wattchow, 2008). This links to broader concepts such as ecological justice. For example, Lily found *storying the outdoors*, (applying Witt, 2017 in practice), supported nature-connection. This workshop introduced place-responsive narrative, engaging participants in storytelling. 'Embodied encounters' along a local river included exploring fairy houses, myths and river ecology, which enabled student teachers to create stories of 'placefulness' (Witt, 2017). Lily explained that 'placemaking' and nature-connection experiences would support children to grow into 'adults who are more likely to be environmentally conscious' with 'real long-term impact'.

Outdoor encounters supported student–teachers to develop a range of personal *connections* and challenge their thinking as they engaged, connected and reflected on new relationships with spaces. Sometimes through drama, roleplay or stories, and, more often as the module developed, recognising the benefits of being *still* in a space. Lily contended that to truly develop the value of place-relationships, pupils should be taken outside 'repeatedly and constantly' and focus on interactions within and beyond that space. She reflected that 'noticing' is a result of feeling comfortable in a space. Person-place connections were described as establishing 'magical moments', where becoming 'engrossed in the environment' and noticing 'smaller details' resulted from engagement with places over time. As Waite (2017) notes, *cumulative* experience, together with reflective practice on experiences that are new and different can result in 'a drastic re-appraisal of what we think we know' (p. 16). In this sense, student–teachers experienced *transformative* processes both on a personal level and as developing professionals.

Student–teachers develop a relationship with OL which facilitates genuine interactions to support their *personal knowledge* (Dubiel, 2023). This enables them to explore different possibilities, work at their own pace, and become more absorbed in an area that interests them and provides them with ownership and autonomy. Student–teachers spoke passionately about creating their own activities and pursuing personal journeys through the module. Relating experiences such as gardening, writing and microteaching, student–teachers connected personal responses, research and subject knowledge to long-term sematic memory: 'I know for a fact that I've now got a lot of Roman knowledge that I'm just not going to forget because I've got ownership of that knowledge and that activity' (Rachel). 'Personal knowledge' was linked by student–teachers to their emerging identities as teachers as experiences shaped the ongoing development of their 'personal teaching philosophy'.

Belonging and participation was reported by student–teachers to be linked to a sense of community and compassion which supported them to overcome barriers to OL. Shared experiences and the supportive group environment motivated and inspired student–teachers to participate during field visits, overcoming barriers such as weather and shyness: 'Everybody just loved it.

They didn't care it was pouring it down' (Amber); 'there was no embarrassment … I didn't feel shy or nervous because everyone was working as a big team … We all want to learn, and we all want to enjoy it' (Rachel). Through repeated group work outdoors, student–teachers overcame initial inhibitions. Emily revealed that she initially 'felt a bit stupid' during a team-building mirror-walk exercise, exploring theories related to place-responsive pedagogy, but with friends guiding her, she 'felt more relaxed'. First-hand experiences in different outdoor settings supported their understanding of considerations such as the impact of noise, traffic and risk. By gaining an understanding of environmental, human and external factors that influence belonging and participation in OL (see Beames et al., 2024 'Supervising People Outdoors' for an excellent guide), student–teachers were able to reflect on their personal experiences on the module to consider how barriers can be overcome.

Learner

Student–teachers' experiences as *learners* inform their beliefs about pedagogy and how children learn outdoors. The module introduces rich opportunities for *experiential learning* and deep engagement with theory in a progressive way, building from theories of early child development through different educational stages, to principles which influence their present development as adults.

Discussing the situative perspective, Lave and Wenger (1991) maintain that learning emerges from and is intertwined with our actions and those of others. Thus, the learner is part of a *community of learning*, within an ongoing 'process of participation' as 'an integral part of generative social practice in the lived-in world' (Lave & Wenger, 1991, p.35). Many student–teachers discussed the group ethos and how personal knowledge, passion and enthusiasm of facilitators had a positive influence on responses to OL. Interviewees reflected on how they learnt from each other. Lara described the benefits of collaboration to get novel ideas from peers: 'People implemented it all differently. … I think it was a big aspect of the module, that you learn a lot from others'. This demonstrates the importance of the social context for learning to take place, cementing a socio-cultural perspective within OL that views 'understanding' not as an 'individual affair (...) but can be seen as being linked more closely to context and experience' (Waite, 2017, p. 17).

Student–teachers narrated different memories of *embodied* experiences in the context of place-responsive pedagogy. Sensory encounters helped them to realise how planning activities to support sensory integration would be highly engaging. Eve reflected on her experience as a 'pupil' during a micro-teach on the Roman Tour of York, where the 'class' made clay figures of Roman soldiers to interact with the place Roman soldiers had once defended. Lara also emphasised the importance of learning about history by 'going to a certain place....to stand where the Romans had once stood'. She noted the groups' engagement and highlighted how powerful this feeling would be for a child. Student–teachers remembered sensorial experiences that impacted their engagement. Rachel recalled how a facilitator fostered student–teacher interests around the theme of 'wonder' during a visit to a local allotment, encouraging them to try edible flowers and herbs. This modelled a flexible, child-centred approach to pedagogy: 'She realised that we were interested so she was just, like give it a go. Try it! I like that flexibility'. Around such practical experiences, facilitators introduced theory about sensorial engagement, prompting student–teachers to reflect on theoretical concepts through which to link their experience within schema. Student–teachers responded to places with awe and wonder, transcending theory normally constrained to Early Years pedagogical approaches (see Chapter 2). By opening themselves up to the opportunities and interactions each place provided, they recognised its unique qualities and value to learning (Woods, 2017, p. 55).

Student–teachers learnt to relate to *pace* through opportunities to attend to the *urgency of the slow* (Clark, 2021) and by experiencing thoughtful, measured approaches to pedagogy. Facilitators enabled time for student–teachers to 'pause or dwell in spaces for more than a fleeting moment' (Payne & Wattchow, 2009, p. 16) and discussed opportunities for attachment, connection, belonging and meaning of place. Several student–teachers discussed how they were initially unsure how the concept of *slow pedagogy* might work in practice within the constraints of the National Curriculum. For example, Emily found the idea of creating an activity from the point of view of a snail 'strange' at first, but after experiencing it for herself, she could see how unhurried facilitation of learning could support children's natural curiosity and 'embrace all of that nature'. Analysis of interviews revealed the deep influence of concepts such as 'follow the child' and 'responsive pedagogy', which were widely praised by student–teachers. Reflecting on her recently completed school practice in Key Stage 2, Lily noted 'it's about the depth and making sure that each child understands and accesses the learning so they can build at their own pace'.

Situated, paced experiences resulted in learning through *play*, where student–teachers constructed their own playful interactions with the outdoors. A key element of ongoing practice was to encourage interactions with different places, with no given outcome. Instinctively, student–teachers engaged in play-based practices, including narrative explorations of the outdoors around 'more-than-human' connections. By 'playing' in different places, student–teachers were able to examine how children will develop 'playful connections with people, places and things' (Woods, 2017). Emily recognised that such first-hand experiences were 'representing how you could do it with children', which broadened her view on practice. Lily said it was a fantastic benefit to 'actually get out and be practical' to experience 'what we would be trying to implement with children'. Many interviewees emphasised play as invaluable to supporting enjoyment and engagement of their learning. Play across the curriculum was also recognised as supporting pupils to overcome barriers. Emily described one activity from the module which involved learning spellings outdoors through teamwork games. She explained that she struggled with spelling throughout primary school and hated spelling tests. But 'if someone had taken me out of that environment and actually made spelling not competitive ... it would have made things so much better'.

Teacher

As a *teacher*, we ask student–teachers to consider how they will enact OL practices as professionals. The module builds in multiple opportunities for them to engage in OL micro-teaches that focus their attention on learning processes, rather than specific curriculum subjects or outcomes. We liken these to Korthagen's *practical, authentic-feeling teaching experiences* (2017). Student–teachers develop a strong understanding of 'context specific, tailored approaches' (Sors & Bloom, 2024) and adaptively respond to learners (their peers) with meaningful interactions. Underpinning this are **holistic and inclusive** values which are communicated throughout the module (see Chapter 3). Eve reflected on the importance of student–teachers working at their own pace and recognised that this would be particularly helpful for pupils with special educational needs and/or disabilities (SEND). Lily concurred, explaining 'it's about responding to the needs of children and allowing...[them] to build their own learning and understanding. That's inherently inclusive because you're meeting the needs of that child'. Emily discussed the benefits of OL for pupils with English as an additional language (EAL). In her teaching practice, she supported pupils with EAL to explore a woodland area, prompting them to communicate with peers and integrate new vocabulary. She noted how outdoor, experiential learning afforded more opportunity for collaboration and argued that experiential approaches were a better way to develop language skills than more abstract methods such showing pupils pictures and words in the classroom. This had been effective because 'they needed the physical connections', encountering vocabulary in real world contexts and learning with and from others through meaningful experiences and engagement with the natural world.

Adaptive and responsive practice was well-understood by student–teachers through their own experiences with facilitators. Lily explained the importance of adapting practice to provide 'opportunities for children to be more central in the learning, so that you can be more child-led and listen to what the children are telling you'. This enables pupils to explore the world in their own time at their own pace to their own level but also highlights the importance of teachers 'stepping back' to support children to develop their own responses to the world around them.

Student–teachers develop **reflexivity** by frequently engaging in formal and informal reflective processes. Often, their reflections give rise to concerns about previous experiences in school settings: for example, schools that rarely employ OL. Such reflections allow facilitators to deepen student–teachers' broader understanding of the different systems in which primary education exists. Interviews with student–teachers *post*-school experience revealed barriers to OL which conflicted with the conviction of its benefits (gestalt) that they had developed through the module. Agendas of performativity within set parameters of 'success' impacted greatly on student–teachers' ability to enact OL in the way they aspired to. Several discussed how academic pressures had a negative impact on them being able to spend time outside with their pupils. Emily reported her class was thought to be 'massively behind' and that the school was under pressure from Ofsted. Consequently, there was a 'huge push' which centred on delivery of prioritised (core) subjects inside classrooms. Lily described how her placement school followed curriculum schemes 'very, very strictly, so there was no deviation', with no possibility to adapt mandated lesson plans to OL. Other barriers such as lack of teacher confidence, access to outdoor spaces, funding and lack of understanding of the value of OL by school leaders and teachers, were also mentioned as impacting on student–teachers enacting OL in practice on school placements.

Many positive examples of *authentic teaching experiences* also illuminated how OL can sit within effectively within curriculum delivery to enhance teacher and pupil engagement. Student–teachers reflected on how using the outdoors put into practice the principles, theory and philosophies they had developed through the module. Emily discussed a science lesson for a Year 3 class, using free-flow investigation of soil outside. She felt that the topic of soil could be quite 'boring' when taught via slide decks in the classroom, but an experiential, slow pedagogical approach outdoors engaged pupils. This embraced ideas of serendipitous 'mudfulness' (see Chapter 5). She described how pupils made connections and explored which types of soil made the best mud bowl, which absorbed the most water and which was the best to paint with. Children were allowed time to become absorbed in the activity and explore different possibilities beyond those defined in 'schemes of learning' or mandated curriculum outcomes. An immersive, curiosity-driven approach resulted in 'intense motivation' through which pupils demonstrated 'flow' (see Chapter 2) and drive to deepen their learning. Student–teachers illustrated examples on how valuing discovery and play had a positive impact on pupils' social and emotional development and wellbeing. One student–teacher explained how she came away from an indoor writing lesson to embrace heavy snowfall, responding to 'children looking out of the window longingly'. She fostered pupils' curiosity by providing cups for them to collect snow outside and observed how they experimented and marvelled as it melted on return to the classroom. In these and other examples, student–teachers played a part in *transformation* and *empowerment* within educational settings, overcoming curriculum pressures. Lily's final thoughts resonated with many interviewees' responses, as she reasoned that all teachers should be trained in OL: 'if more teachers had that passion to implement [OL], the more sway they would have with senior leaders in school who could help decide the curriculum. It works its way up from the bottom up to the top ... I think we need to push for just going outside'.

Conclusion

Student–teacher learning is relational (within social contexts), temporal (framed through previous experiences, influencing new experiences), and situational (grounded in circumstance) (Clandinin & Connelly, 2004). This chapter described an integrated view of teacher learning in the outdoors, to which this can be applied. A 'situative' perspective points towards the need for a focus in OL education and training on the organisation of space, time and opportunity for social interactions in different places. Sharing experiences, dialogic practice and reflection grounded in experiences past, present and future develop personal and pedagogical gestalt. This supports student–teachers to relate schematisation within practice and supports theory formation which will remain a central part of teachers' professional philosophy and practice. Theoretical notions are not so much aimed at building academic knowledge (Theory-with-a-capital-T (Korthagen et al. 2001)), but at deepening and structuring *gestalts* and developing *schemata* characterised by *practical knowledge* that guides perception and action in practice. It requires translation and adaptation of theory to the specifics of each situation. For teacher-educators, drawing on Korthagen's philosophy, the fundamental question becomes: what kind of genuine, situated experiences can be organised that will both effectively shape student–teachers' gestalts and serve as a good starting point for reflection for the development of schemata? This highlights the importance of practice in ITE that is not centred on 'transmission of knowledge and skills, but as an act of (re)directing the attention of students to the world, so that they may encounter what the world is asking from them' (Biesta, 2021, abstract).

The approach taken by the OL module exemplified in this chapter implies a significant shift from traditional HE practices which present theories of learning within isolated courses, which is pedagogically at odds with genuine teaching practice. Cognitive approaches which value academic outcomes persist. Other outcomes in HE require attention, with student perspectives offering insight to ITE providers about how learning through experience can support development of a robust and holistic personal teaching philosophy. Experiential and interactive approaches support personal and professional knowledge development, establishing authentic connections relating to 'real-life' demands of teaching (Korthagen, 2017). Student–teachers' cultural, social and professional capital develops through experiences that shape values and interactions and inform relationships with places and people.

A clear outcome of place-responsive pedagogy in OL is that it presents opportunities for teachers to offer 'education to address the planet's big challenges' (Beames et al., 2024, p. 1), situating pedagogy within critical global issues. This links explicitly to notions of social and environmental justice in terms of what the 'world' is demanding of future teachers. This points towards the need for *realistic* teacher education programmes which include opportunities to foster place-responsive, situated pedagogy and sustainable education to support teachers to respond to the needs and concerns of future generations.

CHAPTER 8

Continuing the Journey of Place-responsive Pedagogy in Outdoor Learning

Ruth Unsworth[a] and Lucy Sors[b]

[a]University of Glasgow, UK
[b]York St John University, UK

Throughout the chapters of this book, contributing authors have explored different facets of how we might build, research and think about outdoor learning (OL) as the lived experience of people and places in educational terms: as *place-responsive pedagogy*. *Place* has been reimagined as a dynamic interconnectedness between people, time, space, ideas and materiality (natural and manmade). *Place connection* as explored in this volume is achieved by viewing places as partners in developing students' conceptual and pragmatic knowledge of the world, through a *world-self-others* relationship. By understanding place and place connection in this way, authors have offered insight into the transformative potential of place-responsive pedagogy within OL. This potential rests on educators developing their own understanding of place(s) and using this understanding to forge interconnectedness between the multifarious components of the world (as both experienced and imagined), the student's self (itself an embodiment of connections and experiences), and others.

Formulation of world-self-other connections has been shown in this book to rely on interactions between external and internal worlds. The interior-exteriority of place entails a reading of place connection and responsiveness as entangled in a complex mix of space(s) and time(s). In the *here-and-now* of present situated activity and simultaneously in the *then-and-there* of embodied lived experience, fragmented into memory and remembrances. This reading of place and place connection shifts the trajectory of 'learning' in discourses of education. We move beyond the 'chalkface' of a learner-centred classroom and curriculum, into interconnected, authentic socio-material experiences. These experiences are curated by teachers to have meaning to the world, and to students' (and others') lives in the world.

Chapters in this book have explored how knowledge and understanding in OL are grounded in social and personal encounters with different places. These encounters are influenced by differing social values, the behaviours of others, and implicit world perspectives embedded in practice. Place-responsive pedagogy thus becomes a journey of 'ways of knowing and states of being' (Adams et al., 2023, p. 23); a path negotiated through multiple external–internal encounters. There is, perhaps, no *end* to this journey, but rather what is of value are the diverse, often surprising, effects of passage: a discovery, a difference made, a penny-drop moment, an episodic memory, a fear overcome, a moment of joy, a friendship forged.

By talking about *place-responsive pedagogy*, we have deliberately not focussed our attention on such words as 'attainment', 'national curriculum' or 'learning outcomes' as markers for progress. OL is, of course, a valuable way of providing real-life experiences for children to access and handle practical examples of abstract concepts in prescribed curricula. We may create stories in woodlands to support writing, conduct scientific, historical or geographical enquiries in local areas, or even teach mathematics through school-situated olive plantations in rural Morocco (CPD College, 2015). However, the kind of education we advocate for starts first and foremost with a *process* of interaction and response between the people, ideas and materials that constitute places. We begin from what is already there and intend to explore it, rather than starting with a list of concepts or subjects to be taught. This book calls for education to focus on direct engagement with the world, and pedagogy that prioritises building connections within, around and beyond it. Children and young people learn about the world through lived responses within and to its places, people, times and problems. Through the idiosyncrasies of personal place response, 'becoming together' (Ingold, 2018) generates a common signification of a place. Through beautiful imaginings and ponderings of interwoven happenings that give back to the world. Through being in comfort zones and uncomfortable zones. Through challenging misconceptions and experiencing the world's uncertainty. Through bravely exploring the dappled shadows of possibility that arise from diverse and unexpected encounters of place.

For the editors of this book, whose childhoods were steeped in neither vast privilege nor rural communities, the outdoors was a place of freedom, learning, entertainment and adventure: our first and enduring teacher. Urban outdoor spaces and encounters with nature taught valuable lessons about the world as we explored its familiarity and remoteness. Spaces of internal quiet were discovered listening to birds in the park: an urban nature. Tarmacked pavements of cramped housing estates offered other possibilities for connecting ideas: that asphalt melts and snapped sticks can create art within it on sticky summer afternoons. Our schools harnessed their playgrounds and fields, nearby scrublands and canal towpaths to provide outdoor encounters and instigate environmental regeneration projects. Gardens, green spaces or countryside rural visits offered spaces to think, to be, to exist in nature. We found places to *play*, our childhoods echoing with the question: 'Are you coming out to play?'. On streets, in parks, or in dens, imagined worlds built with friends in scraps of suburban woodland. We found connections and experienced disconnections. We built lasting relationships with and within the outdoors. Against increased pressures from relentless building on green spaces, the seep of technologisation (O'Connor, 2021) and demands of performative education agendas, we share our conviction of OL as a 'good thing' that is (and should be) accessible to *all* children. Integrating OL into education is not only about group hikes into rolling hills, nor should its discourse be centred around a prevailing rebuttal of OL as part of a privileged education. It is, in our eyes, a pedagogical approach that answers the loss of outdoor childhoods and challenges the indoorisation of education. It establishes a 'sense of place' to be(come) oneself in the/our world(s).

This does not mean that OL should be approached as a one-size-fits-all pedagogy. In fact, we argue the complete opposite in this book. That is, OL necessarily begins with expanding our *own* (practitioner/researcher) knowledge of the *places* we intend to weave educational practice from/within and the *people* who interact within them and bring them into being. This means exploring the plurality of possible connections to be made with, in and to each place in its complex spatio-temporality. Our stance echoes an important direction being taken in education research. Since collating and writing for this volume, we have been inspired by works additional to the research contained within it. One such source of inspiration is Vyas and Dalvi's (2024) critique of the 'greening' movement in concrete suburban Mumbai, which argues for a pluralistic envisioning of what 'greening' means in different (rural/urban) places (Vyas & Dalvi, 2024). Such research points to a future for discourses of OL and place-responsive pedagogy that connects consideration of practice across different communities internationally. We are all tangling with conflicts and desires emergent from a burgeoning international drive to address sustainable development. Education of future generations depends partly on the ways that educators can work together within and without national boundaries, towards ecological approaches which prioritise a global community and the protection of the earth upon which it relies.

With the rise of focus in education research on re-worlding education (Biesta, 2021), we must ask why this focus is so pertinent today. What it is that we have forgotten about the world in today's education systems? In remembering our connections to the world, our communities, our localities and our histories, we look to the wisdom inherent in other approaches to education which place value on sustainability, networks and intergenerational learning. Strength can be drawn from our encounters with and within different places. Encounters that guide us to build the connections needed to respond to evolving existential concerns. This is not regressive (a return to 'what we have lost').

Rather our gaze looks forward, to new connections and interrelationships with the world that address the detrimental impact of the Anthropocene.

We hope that educators, no matter the age of students they teach, will take away from this book ways of thinking about and practising place-responsive pedagogy in the outdoors. We hope readers find inspiration, modes of thought and practical ideas that are not prescriptive, but rather springboards to further thinking and further practices. An important part of the future of education is the research that ponders, probes and questions it. We hope that other researchers take up ideas within this book to 'plough' further into the field of education, growing from the seeds we have planted around place-responsive pedagogy and OL.

References

Abram, D. (1996). *The spell of the sensuous: Perception and language in a more-than-human world*. Vintage Books.
Adams, D. (2023). Cynefin – Being of place. An investigation into the perspectives of first-language Welsh-speaking hill farmers into the meaning of the word cynefin and the significance for education in Wales and beyond. *Journal of Outdoor and Environmental Education, 27*(3), 469–488.
Adams, D., Lewis, R., & Haughton, C. (2023). Bee-ing and feeling of place. In E. Rawlings Smith & S. Pike (Eds.), *Encountering ideas of place in education: Scholarship and practice in place-based learning* (pp. 13–25). Taylor and Francis.
Agnew, J. (1987). *Place and politics: The geographical mediation of state and society*. Routledge.
Ainscow, M. (2007). Taking an inclusive turn. *Journal of Research in Special Educational Needs, 7*(1), 3–7. https://doi.org/10.1111/j.1471-3802.2007.00075.x
Ainscow, M. (2024). *Developing inclusive schools: Pathways to success*. Routledge.
Akram, S. (2023). *Bourdieu, habitus and field: A critical realist approach*. Palgrave Macmillan.
Allen, K. A., Kern, M. L., Rozek, C. S., McInereney, D., & Slavich, G. M. (2021). Belonging: A review of conceptual issues, an integrative framework, and directions for future research. *Australian Journal of Psychology, 73*(1), 87–102.
Anderson, J. (2021). *Understanding cultural geography: Places and traces*. Routledge.
Appadurai, A. (Ed.). (1988). *The social life of things: Commodities in cultural perspective*. Cambridge University Press.
Ardelean, A., Smith, K., & Russell, W. (2021). *The case for play in schools: A literature review*. The-Case-For-Play-In-Schools-web-1-1.pdf (outdoorplayandlearning.org.uk)
Bacharach, B., & David, H. (1957). *Magic moments* [Recorded by P. Como]. RCA Victor.

Baines, E., & Blatchford, P. (2019). *School break and lunch times and young people's social lives: A follow-up national study*. UCL Institute of Education.

Baines, E., & Blatchford, P. (2023). The decline in breaktimes and lunchtimes in primary and secondary schools in England: Results from three national surveys spanning 25 years. *British Educational Research Journal, 49*, 925–946.

Ball, S. (2008). Performativity, privatisation, professionals and the state. In B. Cunningham (Ed.), *Exploring professionalism*. Institute of Education, University of London.

Ball, S. J. (2013). *Foucault, Power, and Education* (1st Ed.). Routledge.

Barrable, A., & Booth, D. (2020). Increasing nature connection in children: A mini review of interventions. *Frontiers in Psychology, 11*, article 492. https://www.frontiersin.org/journals/psychology/articles/10.3389/fpsyg.2020.00492

Barrable, A., & Lakin, L. (2016). Nature relatedness in student teachers, perceived competence and willingness to teach outdoors: An empirical study. *Journal of Adventure Education and Outdoor Learning, 20*(3), 189–201. https://doi.org/10.1080/14729679.2019.1609999

Barrable, A., Touloumakos, A., & Lapere, L. (2022). Exploring student teachers' motivations and sources of confidence: The case of outdoor learning. *European Journal of Teacher Education, 45*(3), 356–372.

Beames, S., Christie, B., & Blackwell, I. (2017). Developing whole school approaches to integrated indoor/outdoor teaching. In S. Waite (Ed.), *Children learning outside the classroom from birth to eleven* (2nd ed.). Sage.

Beames, S., Higgins, P., Nicol, R., & Smith, H. (2024). *Outdoor learning across the curriculum: Theory and guidelines for practice*. Routledge.

Bianchi, L., & Feasey, R. (2011). *Science beyond the classroom boundaries for 3-7 year olds*. Open University Press.

Biesta, G. (2010). *Good education in an age of measurement: Ethics, politics, democracy*. Paradigm Publishers.

Biesta, G. (2017). *The rediscovery of teaching*. Routledge.

Biesta, G. (2021). *World-centred education: A view for the present*. Routledge.

Biesta, G. (2023). Putting the world in the centre: A different future for Scotland's education. *Scottish Educational Review*, 1–21. https://doi.org/10.1163/27730840-20231001

Biesta, G. (2025). The double intervention of world-centred education: Introduction to a book symposium. *Policy Futures in Education, 23*(3), 536–538. https://doi.org/10.1177/14782103251320819

Biesta, G., & Priestley, M. (2013). Capacities and the curriculum. In M. Priestley & G. Biesta (Eds.), *Reinventing the curriculum: New trends in curriculum policy and practice* (pp. 35–49). Bloomsbury.

Boerman, S. C., Meijers, M. H. C., & Zwart, W. (2022). The Importance of Influencer-Message Congruence When Employing Greenfluencers to Promote Pro-Environmental Behavior. *Environmental Communication, 16*(7), 920-941.

Booth, T., & Ainscow, M. (2002). *Index for inclusion: Developing learning and participation in schools.*

Booth, T., & Ainscow, M. (2011). *Index for inclusion: developing learning and participation in schools.* Centre for Studies on Inclusive Education.

Bourdieu, P. (1977). *Outline of a theory of practice.* Cambridge University Press.

Bourdieu, P. (1984). *Distinction: A social critique of the judgment of taste.* Harvard University Press.

Bourdieu, P. (1985). The social space and the genesis of groups. *Social Science Information, 24*(2), 195–220.

Bourdieu, P., & Passeron, J.-C. (1990). *Reproduction in education, society and culture* (2nd ed.) (R. Nice, Trans.). Sage Publications.

Bradley, M., Isaacs, B., Livingston, L., Nasser, D., True, A. M., & Dillane, M. (2011). Maria Montessori in the United Kingdom: 100 years on. In L. Miller & L. Pound (Eds.), *Theories and approaches to learning in the early years.* Sage.

Bronfenbrenner, U. (1994). Nature-nurture reconceptualized in developmental perspective: A bioecological model. *Psychological Review, 101*(4), 568–586.

Bronfenbrenner, U. (1995). Developmental ecology through space and time: A future perspective. In P. Moen, G. H. Elder, Jr., & K. Lüscher (Eds.), *Examining lives in context: Perspectives on the ecology of human development* (pp. 619–647). American Psychological Association. https://doi.org/10.1037/10176-018

Bronfenbrenner, U., & Morris, P. A. (1998). The ecology of developmental processes. In W. Damon (Series Ed.) & R. M. Lerner (Vol. Ed.), *Handbook of child psychology: Vol. 1. Theoretical models of human development* (5th ed., pp. 993–1028). Wiley.

Brookes, A. (2002). Lost in the Australian bush: Outdoor education as curriculum. *Journal of Curriculum Studies, 34*(4), 405–425.

Bruce, T. (2011). *Early childhood education* (5th ed.). Hodder Education.

Casey, E. (1997). *The fate of place: A philosophical history*. University of California Press.

Center for Applied Special Technology (CAST). (2024). *Universal design for learning guidelines version 3.0*. https://udlguidelines.cast.org

Chawla, L. (1990). Ecstatic places. *Children's Environments Quarterly*, 7(4) 18–23.

Children's Alliance. (2021). *The health and wellbeing of children in the early years*. WG1-EarlyYears-Oct2021.pdf (childrensalliance.org.uk)

Christie, B., Higgins, P., & Nicol, R. (2016). Curricular outdoor learning in Scotland: From practice to policy. In B. Humberstone et al. (Eds.), *Routledge international handbook of outdoor studies*.

Clandinin, J. D., & Connelly, M. (2004). Knowledge, narrative and self-study. In J. J. Loughran, M. L. Hamilton, V. K. LaBoskey, &, T. Russell (Eds.), *International handbook of self-study of teaching and teacher education practices. Springer international handbooks of education* (Vol. 12). Springer.

Clark. A. (2021). *Slow pedagogies, slow knowledge and the unhurried child: Time for slow pedagogies in early childhood education*. Froebel Trust Conference Webinar. https://www.froebel.org.uk/research-library/slow-knowledge-and-the-unhurried-child-time-for-slowpedagogies-in-early-childhood-education

Clark, A. (2023). *Slow knowledge and the unhurried child: Time for slow pedagogies in early childhood education*. Routledge.

Clements, R. (2004). An investigation of the status of outdoor play. *Contemporary Issues in Early Childhood*, 5(1), 68–80.

Colman, D. R. (2006). The three princes of Serendip: Notes on a mysterious phenomenon. *McGill Journal of Medicine: MJM*, 9(2), 161–163.

Cooper, S. (2017). *Participatory evaluation in youth and community work: Theory and practice*. Routledge.

Cosgriff, M. (2017). The rewards of professional change: Two primary school teachers' experiences of transforming outdoor education. *Teachers and Curriculum*, 17(1), 23–29.

CPD College. (2015). *Teacher's TV: Where maths grows on trees*. https://www.youtube.com/watch?v=4OaHLlRy7Cc

Cree, J., & Robb, M. (2021). *The essential guide to forest school and nature pedagogy*. Routledge.

Cudworth, D. (2018). Space, place and social relations. In D. Cudworth (Ed.), *Schooling and travelling communities: Exploring the spaces of educational exclusion* (pp. 93–129). Palgrave Macmillan.

Cudworth, D., & Lumber, R. (2021). The importance of Forest School and the pathways to nature connection. *Journal of Outdoor and Environmental Education*, 24, 71–85. https://doi.org/10.1007/s42322-021-00074-x

Davis, J. M., & Elliott, S. (2004). Mud pies and daisy chains: Connecting young children and nature. *Every Child*, 10(4), 4–5.

Decuypere, M., Hartong, S., & van de Oudeweetering, K. (2022). Introduction – Space-and time-making in education: Towards a topological lens. *European Educational Research Journal*, 21(6), 871–882.

Department for Education. (2010). *The Importance of Teaching: The Schools White Paper 2010*. https://assets.publishing.service.gov.uk/media/5a7b4029ed915d3ed9063285/CM-7980.pdf

Department for Education (DfE). (2011–2021). *Teachers' standards: Guidance for school leaders, school staff and governing bodies*. https://assets.publishing.service.gov.uk/media/61b73d6c8fa8f50384489c9a/Teachers__Standards_Dec_2021.pdf

Department for Education. (2014). *National curriculum in England: Framework for key stages 1 to 4*. GOV.UK (www.gov.uk)

Department for Education. (2018–2023). *Working together to safeguard children*. https://assets.publishing.service.gov.uk/media/669e7501ab418ab055592a7b/Working_together_to_safeguard_children_2023.pdf

Department for Education. (2022). *SEND review: Right support, right place, right time government consultation on the SEND and alternative provision system in England*. https://assets.publishing.service.gov.uk/media/624178c68fa8f5277c0168e7/SEND_review_right_support_right_place_right_time_accessible.pdf

Department for Education. (2023). *Special educational needs and disabilities (SEND) and alternative provision (AP) improvement plan: Right support, right place, right time*. https://assets.publishing.service.gov.uk/media/63ff39d28fa8f527fb67cb06/SEND_and_alternative_provision_improvement_plan.pdf

Department for Education. (2024a). *Early years foundation stage statutory framework (EYFSF) Statutory framework for the early years foundation stage for group and school providers* (publishing.service.gov.uk)

Department for Education. (2024b). *ITT core content framework*. https://assets.publishing.service.gov.uk/media/6061eb9cd3bf7f5cde260984/ITT_core_content_framework_.pdf

Department for Education and Department of Health. (2015). *Special educational needs and disability code of practice: 0 to 25 years*. https://www.gov.uk/government/publications/send-code-of-practice-0-to-25

Department for Education and Skills (DfES). (2006). *Learning outside the classroom manifesto.* https://oeapng.info/downloads/download-info/2-2a-lotc-manifesto-publication/

Deringer, S. A., Hodges, J. S., & Griffin, K. (2020). Mindfulness as a tool for place-based educators. *Journal of Outdoor and Environmental Education, 23,* 121–135.

Deroy, O. (2020). Chapter 18: Evocation: How mental imagery spans across the senses. In A. Abraham (Ed.), *The Cambridge handbook of the imagination* (pp. 276–290). Cambridge University Press.

Dewey, J. (1938). *Experience and education.* Collier Books.

Dickinson, E. (2013). The misdiagnosis: Rethinking "Nature-deficit Disorder." *Environmental Communication, 7*(3), 315–335. https://doi.org/10.1080/17524032.2013.802704

Di Renzo, M., Guerriero, V., Zavattini, G., Petrillo, M., Racinaro, L., Bianchi, F., et al. (2020). Parental attunement, insightfulness, and acceptance of child diagnosis in parents of children with autism: Clinical implications. *Frontiers in Psychology, 11,* 1849. https://doi.org/10.3389/fpsyg.2020.01849

Donaldson, G. W., & Donaldson, L. E. (1958). Outdoor education a definition. *Journal of Health, Physical Education, Recreation, 29*(5), 17–63.

Dubiel, J. (2023). *It's not really about dinosaurs… It's not really about dinosaurs* (thevoiceofearlychildhood.com).

Ducarme, F. (2021). *What is nature? Encyclopedia of the environment.* https://www.encyclopedie-environnement.org/en/life/what-is-nature/

Dundon, R. (2023). *A therapist's guide to neurodiversity affirming practice with children and young people.* Jessica Kingsley Publishers.

Dunlap, J. & Kellert, S. R. (Eds.). (2012). *Companions in wonder: Children and adults exploring nature together.* The MIT Press.

Edgington, U. (2016). Performativity and accountability in the UK education system: A case for humanness. *Pedagogy, Culture & Society, 24*(2), 307–312.

Education Endowment Foundation. (2021). *Special Educational Needs in Mainstream Schools.* https://educationendowmentfoundation.org.uk/education-evidence/guidance-reports/send

Education Scotland. (2011). *Outdoor learning: Practical guidance, ideas and support for teachers and practitioners in Scotland.*

Elliott, S., & Davis, J. M. (2020). Challenging taken-for-granted ideas in early childhood education: A critique of Bronfenbrenner's ecological systems theory in the age of post-humanism. In A. Cutter-Mackenzie-Knowles et al. (Eds.), *Research handbook on childhood nature.* Springer.

Engel, G. L. (1977). The need for a new medical model: a challenge for biomedicine. *Science, 196*(4286), 129-36. https://doi.org/10.1126/science.847460

Ernst, J. (2013). Early childhood educators' use of natural outdoor settings as learning environments: An exploratory study of beliefs, practices, and barriers. *Environmental Education Research, 20*(6), 735–752. https://doi.org/10.1080/13504622.2013.833596

Finney, C. (2014). *Black faces, white spaces: Reimagining the relationship of African Americans to the great outdoors*. University of North Carolina Press.

Flanders, M., & Swann, D. (1957). *Hippopotamus*. EMI/Parlophone.

Forest School Association (FSA). (2025). What is forest school? Forest School Association. https://forestschoolassociation.org/what-is-forest-school/

Freire, P. (1996). *Pedagogy of the oppressed*. Penguin Books.

Freire, P. (1998). *Pedagogy of freedom: Ethics, democracy, and civic courage*. Rowman & Littlefield.

Froebel Trust. (n.d.). https://froebel.org.uk/

Froebelian Futures. (n.d). *Moray house school of education and sport*. University of Edinburgh. https://www.froebel.ed.ac.uk/froebel-an-introduction/

Fruin, H. (2020). Muddy play. *YC Young Children, 75*(1), 68–75.

Gabi, J., Olsson Rost, A., Warner, D., & Asif, U. (2023). Decolonial praxis: Teacher educators' perspectives on tensions, barriers, and possibilities of anti-racist practice-based initial teacher education in England. *The Curriculum Journal, 34*, 83–99.

Garden, A. (2022). The case for space in the co-construction of risk in UK forest schools. *Education 3-13, 51*(8), 1281–1292. https://doi.org/10.1080/03004279.2022.2066148

Geertz, C. (1998). *Deep hanging out*. The New York Review of Books.

General Teaching Council Scotland. (GTCS). (2021). *Professional Standards 2021*. https://www.gtcs.org.uk/documents/professional-standards-side-by-side-comparison

Gilead, T. (2012). Education and the logic of economic progress. *Journal of Philosophy of Education, 46*(1), 113–131.

Gourlay, L. (2023). Review of Gert Biesta (2022). World-Centred Education: A View for the Present. *Postdigital Science and Education, 5*, 971–975.

Grant, H., Weale, S., Gregory, A., & Adams, R. (2024). Children facing 'brutal loss' of time and space for play in state schools. *The Guardian*. https://www.theguardian.com/education/article/2024/jun/17/children-facing-brutal-loss-time-space-play-state-schools

Gray, D. (2017). *Empathy map worksheet.* https://xplane.com/worksheet/empathy-map-worksheet/

Gray, T., & Mitten, D. (2018). *The Palgrave international handbook of women and outdoor learning.* Palgrave Macmillan.

Gray, T., & Thomson, C. (2016). Transforming environmental awareness of students through the arts and place-based pedagogies. *Learning Landscapes, 9*(2), 239–260.

Grossman, P., Compton, C., Igra, D., Ronfeldt, M., Shahan, E., & Williamson, P. W. (2009). Teaching Practice: A Cross-Professional Perspective. *Teachers College Record, 111*(9), 2055–2100.

Gruenewald, D. A. (2003). The best of both worlds: A critical pedagogy of place. *Educational Researcher, 32*(4), 3–12.

Gruenewald, D. A. (2008). Place-based education: Grounding cultural responsive teaching in geographical diversity. In D. A. Gruenewald & G. A. Smith (Eds.), *Place-based education in the global age: Local diversity* (pp. 137–153). Routledge.

Guardino, C., Hall, K. W., Largo-Wight, E., & Hubbuch, C. (2019). Teacher and student perceptions of an outdoor classroom. *Journal of Outdoor and Environmental Education, 22*(2), 113–126. https://doi.org/10.1007/s42322-019-00033-7

Hackett, A., & Rautio, P. (2019). Answering the world: Young children's running and rolling as more-than-human multimodal meaning making. *International Journal of Qualitative Studies in Education, 32*(8), 1019–1031.

Hammond, E. (a.k.a @NeuroWild_) (2024). *The NeuroWild shift.* www.teacherspayteachers.com/browse?search=neurowild

Harris, F. (2018). Outdoor learning spaces: The case of forest school. *Area, 50*(2), 222–231.

Hart, R. (1992). *Children's participation: From tokenism to citizenship.* UNICEF Innocenti Research Centre.

Hartig, T., Mang, M., & Evans, G. W. (1991). Restorative effects of natural environment. *Experiences, Environment and Behavior, 23*, 3–27.

Harvey, D. (1996). *Justice, nature and the geography of difference.* Blackwell Publishers.

Hawxwell, L. (2019). You only need a potato peeler and tarpaulin – Perceptions of outdoor learning from primary education trainees. *TEAN Journal, 11*(1), 106–115.

Hawxwell, L., O'Shaughnessy, M., Russell, C., & Shortt, D. (2019). 'Do you need a kayak to learn outside?': A literature review into learning outside the classroom. *Education 3-13, 47*(3), 322–332.

Hayes, T. (2015). A playful approach to outdoor learning: Boggarts, bears and bunny rabbits! In J. Horton & B. Evans (Eds.). *Play, recreation, health and well being*, Vol. 9 of T. Skelton (Ed.), *Geographies of children and young people*. Springer.

Hayes, T. A. (2017a). *Making sense of nature: A creative exploration of young people's relationship with the natural environment* [Unpublished PhD thesis]. University of Cumbria, UK.

Hayes, T. A. (2017b). Kindness: Caring for self, others and nature – Who cares and why? In J. Horton & M. Pyer (Eds.), *Children, young people and care*. Taylor Francis.

Hayes, T. A. (2020). We're all in the wild: Inclusive, creative ways to support young people to discover local outdoor spaces. *Impact*. Chartered College. https://my.chartered.college/author/tracy-ann-hayes/

Hayes, T. A., & Leather, M. (2020). *The Importance of Nature: before, during and after Covid-19*. Part of series: The Impact of Covid-19. [Podcast] 8 July 2020. Available at: https://www.bera.ac.uk/media/the-importance-of-nature-before-during-and-after-covid-19

Hayes, T. A., & Murphy, C. (2022). Searching for fairies outdoors. *Horizons*, 97, 34–38.

Hayes, T. A., & Prince, H. (2019). Shared-story approaches in Outdoor Studies: the HEAR (Hermeneutics, Auto/Ethnography and Action Research) 'listening' methodological model. In B. Humberstone & H. Prince (Eds.), *Research Methods in Outdoor Studies* (pp. 153–163). Routledge.

Hayes, T. A., Leather, M., & Passy, R. (Eds.). (2021). *Wellbeing and being outdoors: BERA Blog Special Issue*. British Educational Research Association. Available at https://www.bera.ac.uk/blog-series/wellbeing-being-outdoors

Hayes, T. A., & Tremble, S. (2022). Magic moments: Noticing magic moments outdoors. *Horizons*, 96, 33–36.

Hayes, T. A., Faulkner, A., & Harris, F. (2016). *Plantlife – We're all in the wild: An inclusive guide to supporting young people with SEN/D to discover their local outdoor spaces*. Wild About Plants. http://insight.cumbria.ac.uk/id/eprint/5829/

Hayes, T. A., Grimwood, S., Leckie, K., & Christie, M. (2022). *Feeling thankful: Therapeutic and educational benefits of agriculture and horticulture*. Social Publishers Foundation Practitioner Research.

Hechter, S. A., & Fife, S. T. (2019). Children and nature. In T. Laszloffy & M. Twist (Eds.), *Eco-informed practice. AFTA Springer briefs in family therapy*. Springer. https://doi.org/10.1007/978-3-030-14954-3_5

Heinemeyer, C. (2022). *BLOG: Learning outside the classroom – And through the living lab*. Institute for Social Justice at York St John University. https://blog.yorksj.ac.uk/isj/2022/11/02/learning-outside-the-classroom-and-through-the-living-lab/

Horseman, L. (2019). How safe is forest school? In M. Sackville-Ford & H. Davenport (Eds.), *Critical issues in forest schools* (pp. 160-173). SAGE Publications Ltd.

House of Commons Children, Schools and Families Committee. (2010). *Transforming education outside the classroom: Sixth report of session 2009-10*. The Stationery Office.

House of Commons Education and Skills Committee. (2005). *Education outside the classroom: Second report of session 2004–05*. The Stationery Office.

House of Lords. (2022). *Children and families 2014 committee report of session 2022-23*. Children and Families Act 2014: A failure of implementation. https://committees.parliament.uk/publications/31839/documents/179148/default/

Hughes, J., Richardson, M., & Lumber, R. (2018). Evaluating connection to nature and the relationship with conservation behaviour in children. *Journal for Nature Conservation, 45*, 11–19.

Hull University. (2023). *QAA inclusive education framework (IEF)*. https://www.qaa.ac.uk/docs/qaa/members/inclusive-higher-education-framework.pdf?sfvrsn=209aaa81_6

Ingold, T. (2013). *Making. Anthropology, archaeology, art and architecture*. Routledge.

Ingold, T. (2017). *Anthropology and/as education*. Routledge.

Ingold, T. (2018). *Anthropology: Why it matters*. Polity Press.

Ingold, T. (2000). *The Perception of the Environment: Essays in Livelihood, Dwelling and Skill*. Routledge.

Institute of Outdoor Learning (IOL). (2024). *Education hub*. https://www.outdoor-learning.org/workforce/ed-hub.html

Isaacs, B. (2012). *Understanding the Montessori approach: Early years in practice*. Routledge.

Jade. (2008). *Kelly kettle*. Woodland Investment Management Limited. https://www.woodlands.co.uk/blog/practical-guides/the-kelly-kettle/

Jimenez, A. C. (2003). On space as a capacity. *The Journal of the Royal Anthropological Institute, 9*(1), 137–153.

Johansson, M. (2006). Environment and parental factors as determinants of mode for children's leisure travel. *Journal of Environmental Psychology, 26*(2), 156–169.

Johnson, J. T. (2012). Place-based learning and knowing: Critical pedagogies grounded in Indigeneity. *GeoJournal, 77*, 829–836. https://doi.org/10.1007/s10708-010-9379-1

Kaplan, S. (1995). The restorative benefits of nature: Toward an integrative framework. *Journal of Environmental Psychology*, *15*(3), 169–182.

Kelly, O. (2022). Outdoor Learning and Student Teacher Identity. In R. Cutting, R and R. Passy (Eds.), *Contemporary Approaches to Outdoor Learning* (Palgrave Studies in Alternative Education). Palgrave Macmillan.

Kelly, O. (2022). Outdoor Learning and Student Teacher Identity. In R. Cutting & R. Passy (Eds.), *Contemporary Approaches to Outdoor Learning*. Palgrave Studies in Alternative Education. Palgrave Macmillan.

Kelly, O., Buckley, K., Lieberman, L. J., & Arndt, K. (2022). Universal design for learning – A framework for inclusion in outdoor learning. *Journal of Outdoor and Environmental Education, 25*, 75–89.

Kemp, N. (2019). Views from the staff room: Forest school in English primary schools. *Journal of Adventure Education and Outdoor Learning*, *20*(4), 369–380.

Kemp, N., & Pagden, A. (2018). The place of forest school within English primary schools: Senior leader perspectives. *Education 3-13, 47*(4), 490–502. https://doi.org/10.1080/03004279.2018.1499791

Khan, M., McGeown, S., Christie, B., & Bell, S. (2023). How can place support pedagogy? Application of the concept of cognitive affordances in research and design of outdoor learning environments. *Landscape Research*, *49*(3), 373–392. https://doi.org/10.1080/01426397.2023.2296490

Korthagen, F. A. J. (2017). A foundation for effective teacher education: Teacher education pedagogy based on theories of situated learning. In D. J. Clandinin & J. Husu (Eds.), *The SAGE handbook of research on teacher education* (pp. 528–544). Sage.

Korthagen, F. A. J., Kessels, J., Koster, B., Lagerwerf, B., & Wubbels, T. (2001). *Linking practice and theory: The pedagogy of realistic teacher education* (1st ed.). Routledge.

Korthagen, F. A. J., & Lagerwerf, B. (2001). 'Teachers' Professional Learning: how does it work?'. In F. A. J. Korthagen (Eds.), *Linking Practice and Theory: The Pedagogy of Realistic Teacher Education*. Routledge.

Lave, J., & Wenger, E. (1991). *Situated learning: Legitimate peripheral participation*. Cambridge University Press.

Learning and Teaching Scotland. (2010). *Curriculum for excellence through outdoor learning*.

Leather, M. (2018). A critique of "Forest School" or something lost in translation. *Journal of Outdoor and Environmental Education, 21*, 5–18.

Lingard, B. (2022). Relations and locations: New topological spatio-temporalities in education. *European Educational Research Journal, 21*(6), 983–993.

Louv, R. (2005). *Last child in the woods: Saving our children from nature-deficit disorder*. Algonquin Books.

Louv, R. (2009). Children and nature-deficit disorder. *Countryside Recreation, 17*(2).

Louv, R. (2010). *Last child in the woods: Saving our children from nature-deficit disorder* (2nd ed.). Atlantic Books.

Louv, R. (2011). *The nature principle: Human restoration and the end of nature-deficit disorder*. Algonquin Books.

Low, S. M. (2009). Towards an anthropological theory of space and place. *Semiotica, 175*, 21–37.

Loynes, C. (2013) Globalization: The market and outdoor adventure. In E. C. J. Pike & S. Beames (Eds.), *Outdoor adventure and social theory* (pp. 135–146). Routledge Taylor & Francis.

Macfarlane, R. (2017). *The lost words*. Hamish Hamilton.

Mainstone-Cotton, S. (2017). *Promoting young children's emotional health and wellbeing: A practical guide for professionals and parents*. Jessica Kingsley Publishers.

Mannion, G., & Lynch, J. (2016). The primacy of place in education in outdoor settings. In B. Humberstone, H. Prince, K. A. Henderson (Eds.), *International handbook of outdoor studies* (pp. 85–94). Routledge.

Mannion, G., Mattu, L. & Wilson, M. (2015). *Teaching, learning, and play in the outdoors: a survey of school and pre-school provision in Scotland*. Scottish Natural Heritage Commissioned Report No. 779.

Marchant, E., Todd, C., Cooksey, R., Dredge, S., Jones, H., Reynolds, D., Stratton, G., Dwyer, R., Lyons, R., & Brophy, S. (2019). Curriculum-based outdoor learning for children aged 9-11: A qualitative analysis of pupils' and teachers' views. *PLoS One, 14*(5), e0212242.

Martin, L., White, M. P., Hunt, A., Richardson, M., Pahl, S., & Burt, J. (2020). Nature contact, nature connectedness and associations with health, wellbeing and pro-environmental behaviours. *Journal of Environmental Psychology, 68*, Article 101389.

Mason, J. (2021). Learning about noticing, by, and through noticing. *ZDM Mathematics Education, 53*, 231–243. https://doi.org/10.1007/s11858-020-01192-4

McDougall, D., Yorke, L., & Hutchinson, S. (2022). *Virtual reality more inclusive fieldwork*. https://fieldwork.wp.worc.ac.uk/wordpress/

Mills, C. (2008). Reproduction and transformation of inequalities in schooling: The transformative potential of the theoretical constructs of Bourdieu. *The British Journal of Sociology of Education, 29*(1), 79–89.

Ministry of Education for New Zealand. (2017). *Te whāriki: He whāriki mātauranga mō ngā mokopuna o Aotearoa Early Childhood Curriculum.* https://www.education.govt.nz/assets/Documents/Early-Childhood/Te-Whariki-Early-Childhood-Curriculum-ENG-Web.pdf

Mol, A., & Law, J. (1994). Regions, networks and fluids: Anaemia and social topology. *Social Studies of Science, 24*(4), 641–671.

Monbiot, G. (2016). *How did we get into this mess? Politics, equality, nature.* Verso.

Munn, N. D. (1992). The cultural anthropology of time: A critical essay. *Annual Review of Anthropology, 21*(1), 93–123.

Muñoz, S.A. (2009). *Children in the outdoors: A literature review.* Sustainable Development Research Centre.

Natural England. (2016). *Natural connections demonstration project, 2012–2016: Final report.* Natural England.

Natural England. (2023). *The people and nature survey for England: Official statistics.* https://www.gov.uk/government/statistics/the-people-and-nature-survey-for-england-adult-data-y3q3-october-2022-december-2022-official-statistics

O'Connor, P. (2021). Introduction. The technologization of the social: A 21st-century megamachine? In P. O'Connor and M.I. Benţa (Eds.), *The technologisation of the social: A political anthropology of the digital machine.* Routledge.

OFSTED. (2008). *Learning outside the classroom: How far should you go?* HMSO.

OFSTED. (2021). *Review and Analysis SEND: Old issues, new issues, next steps.* https://www.gov.uk/government/publications/send-old-issues-new-issues-next-steps/send-old-issues-new-issues-next-stepsPayne.

OFSTED. (2024). *School inspection handbook.* https://www.gov.uk/government/publications/school-inspection-handbook-eif/school-inspection-handbook-for-september-2023

Oglivie, K. (2013). *Roots and wings: A history of outdoor education and outdoor learning in the UK.* Russell House.

Packham, C. (2018). *Autism and me.* Documentary by the British Broadcasting Cooperation (BBC).

Parsons, K. J., & Traunter, J. (2020). Muddy knees and muddy needs: Parents perceptions of outdoor learning. *Children's Geographies, 18*(6), 699–711.

Payne, P. G., & Wattchow, B. (2008). Slow pedagogy and placing education in post-traditional outdoor education. *Journal of Outdoor and Environmental Education, 12*, 25–38.

Payne, P. G., & Wattchow, B. (2009). Phenomenological deconstruction, slow pedagogy, and the corporeal turn in wild environmental/outdoor education. *The Canadian Journal of Environmental Education, 14*(1), 15–32.

Pelias, R. J. (2004). *A methodology of the heart: Evoking academic and daily life*. Altamira

Pettersen, K. (2024). More-than-human and more-than-digital collecting among young children in Norway. *Children's Geographies, 22*(3), 416–430.

Plum, M. (2018). Signing in: Knowledge and action in nursery teaching. *Ethnography and Education, 13*(2), 204–217.

Price, P. (2013). Place. In N. C. Johnson, R. H. Schein, & J. Winders (Eds.), *The Wiley-Blackwell companion to cultural geography*. John Wiley & Sons, Ltd. (pp. 118–129).

Prince, H., & Diggory, O. (2023). Recognition and reporting of outdoor learning in primary schools in England. *Journal of Adventure and Outdoor Learning, 24*(4), 553–565. https://doi.org/10.1080/14729679.2023.2166544

Pritchard, A., Richardson, M., Sheffield, D., et al. (2020). The relationship between nature connectedness and eudaimonic well-being: A meta-analysis. *Journal of Happiness Studies, 21*, 1145–1167.

Pyle, R. M. (1993). *The thunder tree: Lessons from an urban wildland*. Houghton Mifflin.

Pyle, R. M. (2003). Nature matrix: Reconnecting people with nature. *Oryx, 37*, 206–214.

Rawlings Smith, E., & Pike, S. (Eds.). (2024). *Encountering ideas of place in education: Scholarship and practice in place-based learning*. Routledge.

Raymond, P. (2019). *Creativity and/or performativity? A critical case study of tensions experienced by pre-service and early career teachers*. Thesis for Doctor of Philosophy York St John University School of Education.

Richardson, M., Dobson, J., Abson, D. J., Lumber, R., Hunt, A., Young, R., & Moorhouse, B. (2020). Applying the pathways to nature connectedness at a societal scale: A leverage points perspective. *Ecosystems and People, 16*(1), 387–401.

Ritchie, J. (2018). Implementing Te Whàriki. In S. Ryan and S. Grieshaber (Eds.). *Practical transformations and transformational *practices: Globalization, postmodernism, and early childhood education* (pp. 109–136). Emerald Group Publishing Limited.

Roberts, J. W. (2018). Re-placing outdoor education: Diversity, inclusion, and the microadventures of the everyday. *Journal of Outdoor Recreation, Education & Leadership, 10*(1), 20–32.

Roberts-Holmes, G., & Bradbury, A. (2015). The 'datafication' of early years pedagogy: 'If the teaching is good, the data should be good and if there's bad teaching, there is bad data'. *Improving Schools, 19*(2), 119–128.

Rodman, M. C. (1992). Empowering place: Multilocality and multivocality. *American Anthropologist, 94*(3), 640–656.

Ross, H., Higgins, P., & Nicol, R. (2007). Outdoor study of nature: Teachers' motivations and contexts. *Scottish Educational Review*.

Saari, A. (2022). Topologies of desire: Fantasies and their symptoms in educational policy futures. *European Educational Research Journal, 21*(6), 883–899.

Sakr, M., & Kaur, V. (2024). Re-imagining the Froebelian influence on early childhood education as a dynamic and ever-changing web of encounters. *Pedagogy, Culture & Society, 32*(4), 923–940.

Sanderud, J. R., Gurholt, K. P., & Moe, V. F. (2021). Didactic sensitivity to children and place: A contribution to outdoor education cultures. *Sport, Education and Society, 27*, 1086–1099.

Schön, D. A. (1987). *Educating the reflective practitioner: Toward a new design for teaching and learning in the professions*. Jossey-Bass.

Scottish Government. (2004). *Curriculum for excellence*. https://education.gov.scot/curriculum-for-excellence/curriculum-for-excellence-documents/.

Scottish Government. (2012/2023). *Learning for sustainability action plan*. https://www.gov.scot/publications/target-2030-movement-people-planet-prosperity/

Scottish Government. (2023). *All learners in Scotland matter – National discussion on education*. https://www.gov.scot/publications/learners-scotland-matter-national-discussion-education-final-report/

Shakespeare, T. (2022). *How can we redefine disability?* The Royal Institution. https://www.rigb.org/explore-science/explore/video/how-can-we-redefine-disability-tom-shakespeare

Skar, M., Gundersen, V., & O'Brien, L. (2016a). Why do children not play in nearby nature? Results from a Norwegian survey. *Journal of Adventure Education and Outdoor Learning, 16*(3), 239–255.

Skar, M., Gundersen, V., & O'Brien, L. (2016b). How to engage children with nature: Why not just let them play? *Children's Geographies*, 14(5) 527–540.

Sobel, D. (2004). Place-based education: Connecting classroom and community. *Nature and Listening*, 4(1), 1–7.

Sobel, D. (2013). *Place-based education: Connecting classrooms and communities*. Routledge.

Soga, M., & Gaston, K. J. (2016). Extinction of experience: The loss of human–nature interactions. *Frontiers in Ecology and the Environment*, 14(2), 94–101.

Soler, J., & Miller, L. (2003). The struggle for early childhood curricula: A comparison of the English Foundation Stage Curriculum, Te Whariki and Reggio Emilia. *International Journal of Early Years Education*, 11(1), 57–68.

Somerville, M., & Powell, S. J. (2019). Thinking Posthuman with mud: And children of the Anthropocene. *Educational Philosophy and Theory*, 51(8), 829–840.

Sors, L., & Bloom, K. (2024). *When 'compassion' is not enough: An argument for adaptive critical pedagogy in higher education.* BERA Blog post. https://www.bera.ac.uk/blog/when-compassion-is-not-enough-an-argument-for-adaptive-critical-pedagogy-in-higher-education

Sparkes, A. (2007). Embodiment, academics and the audit culture: A story seeking consideration. *Qualitative Research*, 7(4), 521–550.

Spence, C., & Deroy, O. (2013). Crossmodal mental imagery. In S. Lacey & R. Lawson (Eds.), *Multisensory imagery*. Springer.

Strong-Wilson, T., & Ellis, J. (2007). Children and place: Reggio Emilia's environment as third teacher. *Theory into practice*, 46(1), 40–47.

Taylor, A. (2013). *Reconfiguring the natures of childhood*. Routledge.

Taylor, A., Pacinini-Ketchabaw, V., & Blaise, M. (2012). Children's relations to the more-than-human world. *Contemporary Issues in Early Childhood*, 13(2), 81–85.

Tough Mudder. (n.d.). *What is tough mudder?* Tough Mudder. https://toughmudder.co.uk/

Tovey, H. (2017). *Bringing the Froebel approach to your early years practice*. Routledge.

Truong, S., Gray, T., & Ward, K. (2016). "Sowing and growing" life skills through garden-based learning to reengage disengaged youth. *Learning Landscapes*, 10(1), 361–385.

Trussler, S., & Robinson, D. (2015). *Inclusive practice in the primary school: A guide for teachers*. Sage.

Tulving, E. (1972). Episodic and semantic memory. In E. Tulving & W. Donaldson (Eds.), *Organization of memory* (pp. 381–403). Academic Press.

Tyrie, J., & Brinn, M. (2024). Can the curriculum for Wales and 'cynefin' enable children's participative rights in schools? In *British Educational Research Association (BERA). Doing cynefin: Exploring ideas on belonging, connectedness and community in the Curriculum for Wales [Blog series]*. https://www.bera.ac.uk/blog/can-the-curriculum-for-wales-and-cynefin-enable-childrens-participative-rights-in-schools

Ulrich, R. S. (1984). View through a window may influence recovery from surgery. *Science*, 224, 420–421.

UNICEF. (2017). Inclusive Education: Understanding Article 24 of the Convention on the Rights of Persons with Disabilities. Retrieved from https://www.unicef.org/eca/sites/unicef.org.eca/files/IE_summary_accessible_220917_0.pdf

United Nations Educational, Scientific and Cultural Organization (UNESCO). (2002–present). *Local and Indigenous Knowledge Systems (LINKS)*. https://www.unesco.org/en/links

UNESCO. (1994, 7–10 June). *The Salamanca Statement and Framework for action on special needs education*. Adopted by the World Conference on Special Needs Education; Access and Quality. Salamanca, Spain.

UNESCO. (2016). *School and teaching practices for twenty-first-century challenges: Lessons from the Asia-Pacific region, regional synthesis report;2014 regional study on transversal competencies in education policy and practice (Phase II)*. https://unesdoc.unesco.org/ark:/48223/pf0000244022

UNESCO. (2020). *Education in a post-COVID world: Nine ideas for public action*. UNESCO.

Unilever. (2024). *Dirt is good. Play on!* Unilever. https://www.persil.com/uk/our-commitments.html

Unsworth, R. (2023). Teaching through the cloud: An ethnography of the role of cloud-based collaborative technologies in the formation of teachers' classroom practices. *Anthropology & Education Quarterly*, 55(1), 24–42.

Unsworth, R. (2024). Place, space and time: A topological perspective of a forest school-based educational mode of existence. *European Educational Research Journal*, 24(3), 327–343.

Valentine, G., Skelton, T., & Chambers, D. (1998). Defining youth. In T. Skelton & G. Valentine (Eds.), *Cool places: Geographies of youth culture*. Routledge.

Vander Ark, T., Liebtag, E., & McClennen, N. (2020). *The power of place: Authentic learning through place-based education.* ASCD.

Vyas, T., & Dalvi, G. (2024). 'No trees around, but we paint some on our walls': Cultivating the 'green' image within schoolscapes in India. *Ethnography and Education*, 1–18. https://doi.org/10.1080/17457823.2024.2407966

Waite, S. (2007). 'Memories are made of this': Some reflections on outdoor learning and recall. *International Journal of Primary, Elementary and Early Years Education, 35*(4), 333–347.

Waite, S. (Ed.). (2017). *Children learning outside the classroom: From birth to eleven* (2nd ed.). Sage.

Waite, S., & Pratt, N. (2017). Theoretical perspectives on learning outside the classroom – Relationships between learning and place. In S. Waite (Eds.), *Children learning outside the classroom: From birth to eleven* (2nd ed.). Sage.

Warren, K., & Breunig, M. (2019). Inclusion and social justice in outdoor education. In M. Peters (Eds.), *Encyclopedia of teacher education.* Springer.

Wattchow, B. (2008). Slow pedagogy and placing education in post-traditional outdoor education. *Journal of Outdoor and Environmental Education, 12,* 25–38.

Wattchow, B., & Brown, M. (2011). *A pedagogy of place: Outdoor education for a changing world.* Monash University Publishing.

Welsh Government. (2022). *Curriculum for Wales guidance.* https://hwb.gov.wales/curriculum-for-wales

Whitehouse, P. (2017). *20 glorious ways to play with mud!* Mother Natured. https://mothernatured.com/nature-play/mud-play-for-kids/

Williams-Siegfredsen, J. (2012). *Understanding the Danish forest school approach.* Abingdon.

Witt, S. (2017). Storying the outdoors. In S. Pickering (Ed.). *Teaching outdoors creatively.* Routledge.

Woods, A. (2017). *Elemental play and outdoor learning: Young children's playful connections with people, places and things.* Routledge.

World Health Organization. (2001). *International classification of functioning, disability and health: ICF.* World Health Organization.

Xia, Y., Wang, P., & Vincent, J. (2024). Why we need neurodiversity in brain and behavioral sciences. *Brain-X, 2,* e70. https://doi.org/10.1002/brx2.70

Zylstra, M. J., Knight, A. T., Esler, K. J., et al. (2014). Connectedness as a core conservation concern: An interdisciplinary review of theory and a call for practice. *Springer Science Reviews, 2,* 119–143.

Index

Abram, D., 24, 38, 48
Academic progress, 42
Access, 21, 61, 114, 145
Accessibility, 65
Active engagement, 22, 62
Active noticing, 54, 61, 66, 74
Activities, 13, 36, 68, 78, 107, 113, 133
Adams, D., 34–35, 44–46, 49–51, 160
Adaptive critical pedagogy, 55
  adaptive practice, 155
  additional and different support, 55
  adjustments, 66–67
Adolescence, 103
Adult(s), 36–37, 104
  adult–child interactions, 36
  adult–child relationships, 39
  guided learning, 40
  modelling, 40
Affective attachment 86
Age-appropriate behaviour, 103
Agency, 26
  individual, 25–26, 54
Agreed boundaries, 64
Ainscow, M., 60
Akram, S., 25–26, 91
Alternative pedagogies, 34
Anthropocene, 60
Anthropocentric approach, 116
Anthropology, 2, 7
Anticipation, 73
Appadurai, A., 18, 30, 85
Artistry in outdoor educational practice, 1

Assessment, 140–141
'Attainment', 160
Authentic
  creativity, 141
  experiences, 37
Autonomy, 47, 49, 59

Baines, E., 40
Banking model of education, 39
Barrable, A., 124–125, 131, 146
Barriers
  to outdoor learning, 124–127
  overcoming/removing barriers, 151, 154
  to participation and learning, 67
  socio-cultural barriers, 52, 145
Beames, S., 120
Behaviour(s), 38, 40, 85, 108, 145, 160
  observable, 74
  professional, 58
Being in place, 48
Beliefs, 40, 85, 94, 152
Belonging, 60, 74, 151
  to and being in world, 48–49
Benefits of outdoor learning
  educational, 101, 106
  emotional, 104, 106, 116–117
  health and well-being, 102–103
  holistic, 40
  therapeutic, 101, 106
Biesta, G., 30, 38
Bio-ecological system, 60
Bio-psycho-social model, 69
Blatchford, P., 40

Body awareness, 13
Booth, T., 57, 146
Boundaried elements of forest, 91
'Boundary-less exploration', 49
Bourdieu, P., 19, 25–26
  capital, 25
  doxa, 47
  field, 25
  habitus, 25
  theory of practice, 25
British Educational Research Association
  BLOG series, 45
  Special Interest Group, 2
Bronfenbrenner, U., 60
  ecological systems theory, 47
Brown, M., 18, 27–29, 66, 68
Bruce, T., 35, 40
Bucket School approach, 119–134

Casey, E., 17, 20
Challenges in outdoor learning, 43, 93
Character of curriculum, 61
Characteristics of effective learning (CoEL), 43
Child
  child-centred pedagogy, 38
  child-centred theories, 38
  childhood experiences, 127
  development, 35–36, 41
Children and Families Act (2014), 57, 59
Christie, B., 124
Clandinin, J. D., 145
Clark, A., 42, 96, 98
'Classroom', 109
  classroom-based learning, 72
  space-time, 85
Co-construction, 78
  in RA, 78
Cognition and learning (CL), 72
Cognitive development, 2
Collaboration, 47
Colonialism, 56

Colonisation, 23
Communication, 115
Community
  community-responsive approach, 47
  eco-systems of, 47–48
  of learning, 152
Compassion, 71
Compassionate pedagogy, 42
Concerns, 119, 121, 126, 155, 158
Confidence, 119–120, 126, 145
Conflicts within English education system, 39–42
Connected pedagogy, 30
Connectedness as key feature of place-responsive OL, 34
Connection(s), 4, 50, 60
  to environment, 74
  to nature, 116
  to place, 37, 68
  to self, 13, 21
Connelly, M., 145
Consultation, 67
Context-responsive approach, 139
Conversations, 145
Cooper, S., 117
Council for Learning Outside the Classroom (CLOtC), 121–122, 125
Creativity, 9, 115, 117
  creative approaches to teaching and learning
  creative educational research
Cree, J., 84
Critical pedagogy, 63, 93
Critical pedagogy of place (Gruenewald), 29
Critical reflection, 55
Crossmodal imagery, 20–21
Cudworth, D., 85, 96, 98
Culture, 7
  cultural capital, 44, 144
  cultural development, 2
  cultural learning, 51

eco-systems of, 47–48
theory, 52
Curiosity approach (Reggio Emilia), 37
Curriculum, National, 41, 122–123, 153, 160
curricula for Wales, 33
curriculum for England, 35
curriculum for excellence (Scotland), 124
curriculum for new Zealand, 44
Cynefin, 45–50

Davis, J. M., 60–63, 106
Decolonising outdoor learning
belonging to and being in world, 48–49
connectedness and responsive curriculum designs, 49–50
eco-systems of community and culture, 47–48
extending EY principles around play, 39–42
Indigenous and local connections to place-responsive OL, 44–47
slow pedagogy and fostering connection, 42–43
theories and perspectives informing place-responsive OL, 34–39
Deliberate approach, 1
Department for Education (DfE), 55
Deroy, O., 20–21
Dewey, J., 38
Dialogic reflection, 147
Dickinson, E., 24
Digital technologies, 23
Disability, 69
Disconnection, 22, 24
Diversity, 6, 50, 70
Donaldson, J., 93
Doxa, 19, 25, 34, 45, 47, 56

Dundon, R., 70
Dynamic learning process, 18

Early childhood, 35, 104
Early Years (EY), 34
Early Years Foundation Stage Framework, 40–41, 43
Eco-systems, 47–48
Ecological relationship, 54
Ecological systems theory, 47
Edgington, U., 97
Education, 3, 6–7, 18, 51, 84, 93, 114, 122
education-focussed research community, 6–7
England, 123–134
policy, 124
research, 162
Scotland, 124
support for OL in, 121–123
Educational
experiences, 30
outcomes, 8–9
philosophy, 8
process, 3
theory, 35, 38
Egologic/Ecologic, 38, 41, 48
Elliott, S., 61, 63, 106
Embodied
experiences, 152
sensory-perceptual factors, 68
Emotion, 89
Empathy, 23
mapping, 74
Empowerment, 71, 156
Encounter, 4
Engagement, 45, 60
with place, 78, 150
English as Additional Language (EAL), 154–155
Environment, 37, 58, 68, 86
environmental connection, 36
environmental education, 2
environmental stewardship, 107

Episodic memory, 21–22
Epistemological lens, 62
Equality, 56
    Equality, Diversity and Inclusion (EDI), 56–57
    Equality Act (2010), 57
Ethnography in education, 88
    ethnographic approaches, 88
    ethnographic enquiry, 7
Experience(s), 5, 21, 40
    experiential connections, 8, 38
    experiential learning, 147, 152
    experiential pedagogy, 38
    explorations of place-responsive pedagogy, 8
    of world, 23
'Experts', 119, 126, 131

Fife, S. T., 24
Finney, C., 56
Flexibility, 79
Fluid spatiality, 88, 96–98
Forest School, 125
    approach, 89–90, 97
    education, 78
    Forest School Association, 89–90
    leader, 126
Fostering connection, 42–43
Four broad areas of need, 72
'Free-flow' in EY curriculum, 40
Freedom, 23, 36, 40, 130, 161
Freire, P., 63
Frilutsliv, 125
Froebel, F., 35
Froebelian principles and vision, 35, 39
Fruin, H., 106, 116

Garden, A., 78
Gardening, 93, 105
Geertz, C., 98
Gestalts, 144
Gray, T., 74
Green space, 109
Grounding activities, 13

Gruenewald, D. A., 29, 54, 93
Gurholt, K. P., 2

Habitus, 19, 25–26, 28, 87, 143–144, 146
    as method, 27
Harris, F., 97
Hart, R., 59
Hawxwell, L.
Hayes, T., 94, 102–103, 106, 110, 113, 115
Health, 69, 102
Healthy risks, 79
Hechter, S. A., 24
Henry, J., 102
Here-and-now perspective, 160
High expectations, 58, 65
Higher education, 140
Holistic approach, 30, 55
    holistic assessment in OL, 67–79
    holistic development, 47
    holistic value, 154
Human-environment relationships
    human nature disconnection, 23
    human-nature (inter) connection, 60
    more-than-human, 24, 38, 60, 74, 113, 115, 153

Imagination, 21, 92
Implicit skills, 3
Imposter syndrome, 119
Inclusion
    inclusive and holistic approach, 30
    inclusive cultures, 59
    inclusive education framework, 141
    inclusive turn (Ainscow, M.), 60–63
    inclusive value, 154
    to meaningful participation, 56–59
    in OL, 63

Indigenous knowledge, 44–45
Individual
  agency, 25–26, 54
  interests, 53
  needs, 59, 70, 122
Indoorisation/Indoorism, 35, 78
Ingold, T., 112
Initial Teacher Education (ITE)
  integrating theory and practice, 143–145
  module design, 145–148
  OL in, 140–142
  student–teachers, 142
Innovative
  teaching-learning, 120
  thinking, 6
Integral skills, 50
Interconnection/Interrelationships, 35, 60–61, 162
Intergenerational learning, 162
Intersectionality, 63
'Interwoven mat', 48
Intrapersonal skills, 6
Isaacs, S., 38

Jimenez, A. C., 86
Joint planning, 65

Kaur, V., 36
Kemp, N., 125–126
Kindergarten, 35, 125
Korthagen, F. A. J., 140
  model of realistic teacher education, 139

Lagerwerf, B., 140
Lave, J., 152
Law, J., 88
Learner(s), 4, 140, 148–149, 152–154
'Learnification', 39
Learning environments, 38, 49, 58
Learning outcomes, 3, 160
Learning Outside the Classroom (LOTC), 2, 54, 121
  manifesto, 54

Leather, M., 135
Lingard, B., 68
Lived experience, 18
Local
  community, 86
  environment, 120
  knowledge, 33, 38, 50
  local-based pedagogies, 44
  priorities, 61
Logic of progress, 41
Louv, R., 24, 107, 126–127
Low, S. M., 86
Lynch, J., 5, 8–9, 18

Macfarlane, R., 126
Macmillan sisters, 38
Malaguzzi, L., 37
Mannion, G., 5, 8–9, 18
Māori understandings of nature connection, 50
'Mapping' place, 73
Marketisation, 17, 97
Mason, J., 54, 61, 66, 80
Materiality of place, 84
  material-memory relationality, 93
Meaningful participation, 56–59
'Meet the world', 39
Memory, 68, 98, 102
  episodic memory, 21
  recall, 21
  semantic memory, 21
Mental health, 2
  benefits, 2
  mental well-being, 106
Metacognition, 141
Microteaching, 151
Mills, C., 44
Mindful(ness), 13, 104
  mindful place-based pedagogy, 13
Ministry of Education New Zealand (MENZ), 44
Moe, V. F., 2
Mol, A., 88

Moments-in-time, 18, 85
Montessori, M., 36–37
More-than-human
  aspect, 74
  ecological approach, 60
  multimodal meaning-making, 113
  relationships, 24
Mud, 92, 102–103
  muddy moments, 101–102, 109–112
  muddy play, 104, 107, 114
  mudfulness, 10, 101–103
  review of literature, 104–109
Multi-modal, 26
Multi-sensory, 26
Multifactorial design, 67
Munn, N. D., 86
Muñoz, S. A., 5

Narrative enquiry, 147
National curriculum, 41, 122–123, 153, 160
National Outdoor Learning Award (NOLA), 125–126
Natural
  environment, 40, 57, 104–105
  materials, 107, 125, 133, 142
  world, 148
Natural England, 121, 125
Nature, 2, 104–105
  connection, 24
  deficit disorder, 24, 109, 127
  definitions of, 104
  disconnection, 24
  nature-based experiences, 107
  as teacher, 35
Nature Survey, 5
Network associations of place, 94–96
Neurodiversity, 71
  neurodivergent identity, 71
  neurodiversity-affirming practice, 70

New Zealand, bicultural nature of, 50
Nonhuman, 60

O'Connor, P., 23, 161
OFSTED, 57
Oglivie, K., 5, 35
Open-ended pedagogy, 90
Oppression, 56
Outcomes-valued schooling, 3
Outdoor education, 2, 28
Outdoor learning (OL), 1–4, 14, 17, 22, 28, 34–35, 44, 58, 102, 110, 120, 124, 140, 159
  barriers to, 124–127
  concept of, 44
  definitions, 2
  inclusive in, 63
  in initial teacher education, 140–142
  integration with place-responsive pedagogy, 6–9, 27–31, 50–52
  overcoming barriers to, 151, 154
  urgency of, 5–6
Outdoor play, 106
Ownership, 40, 49

Packham, C., 70–71
Participation, 151
Partnerships, 43
Passeron, J. C, 26, 34, 41, 44, 61
Payne, P. G., 68
Pedagogy, 18, 69, 120
  pedagogic action, 41
  pedagogical design, 53
  place-responsive, 6–9, 27–31, 50–52
Performativity, prevalence of, 39
Personal
  connection, 140, 151
  development, 121
  knowledge, 151

person-place connections, 151
responsive approaches, 54
teaching philosophy, 151–158
Person–learner–teacher, 148–149
Physical
  education, 108, 123
  well-being, 106
  wellness, 2
Physiological needs, 74
Pike, S., 83, 85
Place
  conceptualisation of, 84
  connection, 86, 88, 98, 159
  disconnection, 88
  learning about, 18
  pedagogy of, 19
  sensitivity to, 68
Place-based pedagogy, 18, 44
  community, 60
  education
  experiences
  learning, 41
Place-responsive pedagogy
  definition and principles, 6–9
  beyond early years, 9, 34
  in planning, 145
  relationship to outdoor
    learning, 6–9, 27–31,
    50–52
  in teacher education, 139
Placemaking, 150
Play, 153, 161
  play-based learning, 40
  play-based pedagogy, 38
  playful adventures outside,
    101
  playfulness, 10
Policies, 58
Positive outcomes, 30
Post-EY practice, 39
Power dynamic/relations, 85
Practical ideas, 163
Practical knowledge, 157
Practitioner inquiry, 143
Pratt, N., 3–4

Pre-emptive planning, 79
Predetermined educational goals,
  34
Price, P., 85
Primacy of place, 9
Primary education, 40, 140
Privilege, 22, 161
Problem-solving, 6
Process, 160
  of education, 7
  of learning, 46
Process, person, time and
  context (PPTC), 61,
  66, 73
Professional artistry, 145
Professional conversations, 73
Proximal process, 61, 69, 144
Pyle, R. M., 85, 108

Qualified Teacher Status (QTS),
  140

Rawlings-Smith, E., 83, 85
Reasonable adjustments, 65
Reconnection, 2
'Reflection-in-action' moments,
  145
Reflections, 4
Reflexive practice, 26
Reggio Emilia approach, 37
Relationship, 84
Remembrances, 92
Responsive(ness), 4, 6–7, 146
  curriculum, 49–50
  to experiences, 3
  pedagogy, 52
  to place, 4
Risk
  risk assessment, 78
  risk-aversion, 78
  risk/benefits, 78
  risky play, 78
Robb, M., 84
Ross, H., 126
Rural and/or urban, 162

Saari, A., 87
Safeguarding, 113
Safety
  safety and belonging, 65, 74–79
  safety and risk, 121
Sakr, M., 36
Sanderud, JR., 2
Schema, 144
Schön, D. A., 145
School grounds, 120
Scottish Government, 124
Sedentary learning experiences, 147
Self-esteem, 72
Semantic memory, 21–22
Sense of place, 98
Senses
  sensorial connection, 21
  sensory experiences, 8
  sensory inputs, 72
  sensory plane, 20
Sensory and physical (SP), 72
Serendipitous encounters with mud, 102
Shakespeare, T., 70
Shared (sharing), 66
  expectations, 65, 78
  experiences, 24, 117, 151
Sites of outdoor learning, 145
Situated learning, 30, 48, 149
Situated pedagogy, 30
Situative perspective, 152
Skar, M., 115
Slow pedagogy, 30, 42–43, 69, 96, 153
Sobel, D., 61
Social, 88
  action, 25
  anthropology, 7
  becoming, 7
  connection, 27
  discourse, 29
  injustice, 145
  justice, 62
  media, 23
  topological lens, 87, 98
  topology, 83, 87–89
  well-being, 106
  work, 67
Social and emotional development, 122
Society, 19, 27, 45
Socio-cultural perspective
  experiences impacting, 23
  social values, 160
  socio-cultural learning, 41
  socio-cultural understandings of place, 7
Soga, M., 108–109
Space, 84
  space, place and time, 84–87
  space-time and reimagining place, 8, 85
  spatio-temporality, 83
Special Educational Needs and Disabilities (SEND), 54–55, 57, 72
Special Educational Needs Code of Practice (SEND CoP), 57, 72
Speech, Language and Communication (SLC), 73
Spiritual experiences, 44
Storying, 28
Storytelling, 92
Strengths, barriers and needs, 69–74
Strengths-based approach, 70
Student-teachers, 146, 151, 153
  reflections, 155
  student voice, 139, 148–149
  student-centred practice, 145
  views, 140
Subject, 51, 61
Sustainability, 162
Symbolic power, 61
Symbolic violence, 34, 41

Targeted support, 9, 65
Taylor, A., 105

Te Whāriki, 44–50
Teacher training in OL
　teacher confidence, 126
　teacher expertise, 119
Teacher(s), 90, 95–97, 131, 140, 148–149, 154–157
Teaching philosophy, 146
Technological expansion, 23
Temporal-spatial details, 21
Theories of learning, 157
Theory-level understanding, 148
Time, 84, 142
　inclusive approaches to, 67–69
　for slow, 43
Tools, 55
Transformation, 61–62, 156
　process of, 124
　transformative learning, 8
　transformative power, 151
　transformative practice, 25
Transparency, 79
Transversal skills, 141
Trust, 57

UNESCO, 6, 44, 56, 141
Unintended learning, 3, 144

'Unity and connectedness', 35
Universal Design for Learning (UDL), 58
Universal support, 55

Value(s), 51, 58, 151
Virtual Field Trips (VFTs), 79
Virtual spaces, 8

Waite, S., 150
Wattchow, B., 68
Well-being, 2, 102, 107
Welsh Government, 45–47, 49–50
Wenger, E., 152
Whole-child development, 34
Working Together to Safeguard Children (WTSC), 67
World-centred education, 6–7, 114
　world-centred vision, 38
　world-connection, 49, 51
　world-self-others relationship, 159
Writing, 123, 151

York St John University, 140

www.ingramcontent.com/pod-product-compliance
Lightning Source LLC
Chambersburg PA
CBHW061939220426
43662CB00012B/1965